Basic Bible Sermons on the Ten Commandments

BASIC BIBLE SERMONS

ON

THE TEN COMMANDMENTS

Jerry Vines

BROADMAN PRESS
NASHVILLE, TENNESSEE

Scripture quotations are from the *King James Version of the Bible* unless otherwise stated.

Scripture quotations marked NIV are from Holy Bible, *New International Version.* Copyright © 1973, 1978, 1984 by International Bible Society.

Scripture quotations marked TLB are from *The Living Bible.* Copyright © Tyndale House Publishers, Wheaton, Illinois, 1971. Used by permission.

Library of Congress Cataloging-in-Publication Data

Vines, Jerry.
    Basic Bible sermons on the Ten commandments / Jerry Vines.
        p.   cm
    Includes bibliographical references.
    ISBN 0-8054-2281-1 :
    1. Ten commandments—Sermons.   2. Bible.   O.T.   Exodus XX, 1–17
—Sermons.   3. Baptists—Sermons.   4. Sermons, American.   I. Title.
BV4655.V56   1992
241.5′2—dc20   91-39552
                                                                                      CIP

To the faithful people of our
First Baptist family, who listened
to these messages on Sunday nights
and constantly challenge me
to give my best

Preface

Exodus is a book of deliverance for the people of God. In it three major spiritual lessons are set forth—how God saves His people (the exodus), how He separates His people (the giving of the Law), and how He satisfies His people through His providential power and protection.

Towering prominently in Exodus is God's atonement for Israel. God delivered them on Passover night by blood and then carried them through the Red Sea. With His redemption, however, there came requirements. God desired His people to be like Him—holy. When Jehovah confronted Moses through the burning bush, He required Moses to remove his shoes, "for the place whereon thou standest is holy ground" (Ex. 3:5b). God demands holiness of His followers: "Ye shall be holy; even as I am holy" (Lev. 11:44). When God saves His people, He sanctifies them, setting them apart. His children are to reproduce Him—His image, His likeness, His behavior, His style. He is Holy God, and He calls for His people to be different from the society around them.

How mistaken multitudes of people are to think that The Ten Commandments can save! The Ten Commandments, of course, form the ethical and moral basis for all our relationships, between God and/or human beings, but they can only point out our shortcomings and sins. Nonetheless, we are to accept them seriously. Many professing Christians have commented, "The Ten Commandments don't make any difference today. We are not under the Law but under grace." But, they do make a difference! Yes, Paul in his Epistles taught that the Law is the schoolmaster, the pedagogue, but it is absolutely vital for the Christian to follow first of all the grace of the Lord Jesus Christ, realizing that Jesus came to fulfill the law, not to do away with it.

"Through the Law alone," writes Donald G. Bloesch, "we can arrive at a knowledge of our guilt, but we cannot have a true perception of our sin. We can be awakened to the burden of our guilt through the Law by itself, but we will not know the enormity of our sins until they are exposed in the light of the cross and resurrection of Jesus Christ."[1]

The Ten Commandments cannot save, but they can day by day aid the believer in his sanctification. Here I relate the Ten Commandments to the gospel of our Lord and Savior Jesus Christ. These Commandments need to be inscribed on our hearts, both the positive and negative aspects. Yes, we are saved by grace, but we are to adhere to the ethical and moral teachings of these foundational Commandments. All of our behavior and interactions are covered in them. My prayer is that these Commandments may mean far more to you than ever before.

> *Jerry Vines*
> *First Baptist Church*
> *Jacksonville, Florida*

Note

1. Donald G. Bloesch, *Essentials of Evangelical Theology* (San Francisco: Harper & Row, 1978), 2 Vols., 1:97.

Contents

1
God and God Alone

(Ex. 20:1-3)

The Ten Commandments are as timely today as ever. They need to be studied in detail and depth since they touch on every problem we face.

The children of Israel had gathered at the foot of Mount Sinai. Moses had gone up into the presence of God, and there the Lord God Jehovah gave Moses the Ten Commandments. The Ten Commandments have been described in a variety of ways by different writers. One author refers to the Ten Commandments as "God's blueprints for living." Another calls them "God's laws for today's godless world." However you describe the Commandments, all of us would agree that they are extremely pertinent and important.

I recently preached a message on the fact that Israel was under the law and New Testament believers are not under the law; we are under grace. I want to make it clear that when we say we are not under the law, that does not mean there are no rules. This is not to suggest that we live in a kind of anything-goes mode. I do not mean that at all. We couldn't have a universe if there were not certain rules—certain fixed standards. There could be no mathematics if there were no laws of mathematics. There could be no physics if there were no laws of physics. All of us understand the importance and the necessity of rules.

Just suppose that next fall or winter you go to the Georgia/Florida football game. You walk in and there are seventy thousand-plus people there. Also suppose the first thing you notice is that there are no boundary lines. You look to your right in the stands, and there is a Georgia player in his uniform, and you ask him, "Who are you?"

He replies, "I'm a wide receiver for the Georgia Bulldogs."

"What are you doing up here?"

"I thought they would have a hard time getting me up here, so I'm here ready to catch a pass." Then you look down the field, and two Florida players have another Georgia player down, and they are beating him up.

You yell, "What in the world are you doing?"

They come back with "This is the quarterback, we're whipping up on him so he won't be able to throw a pass." Then the whistle blows, the game starts, and people are running in all directions. Players are kicking field goals, and others are throwing passes. You are going to have an interesting, but confusing, afternoon.

I'm dealing with absurdity because you realize you cannot have a football game without rules. Rules are absolutely essential. So, the Ten Commandments are God's divine principles which underlie moral society. The question before us is: Are these Ten Commandments out of date? Have we gone past these Ten Commandments? From time to time when you make mention of the Ten Commandments, you hear people use words like *outmoded*, or *out of date*. Some time ago, Ted Turner, who owns several cable television networks, was speaking to a group of broadcasters. In his speech he observed that the Ten Commandments are out of date. Mr. Turner modestly offers to replace the Ten Commandments with his own version, which he calls the "Ten Voluntary Initiatives." The first: I love and respect planet Earth and all living things thereon, especially my fellow species—mankind. The second: I promise to treat all persons everywhere with dignity, respect, and friendliness.

That was the same speech, by the way, where he bashed Christians and called them "losers." It was the same speech where he said, "I don't want anybody to die for me." It's the same speech where he called Christians "bozos." Later he apologized for his remarks about Christians. He has not yet apologized, to my knowledge, to the Lord God for trying to undo His Ten Commandments. Ted Turner is representative of the society in which we live—those who claim that the Ten Commandments given to Moses on Mount Sinai are out of date, we've gone past them in our day, and they are no longer necessary.

The truth of the matter is we have not gone past the Ten Commandments. We haven't caught up to them yet! The Ten Commandments were not only given by God on tablets of stone, but the Bible teaches they have been engraved somewhere else. In Romans 2:15 we read that the law of God has been written on the heart—the human conscience. Down inside, mankind has an understanding that the Ten Commandments are not obsolete, but rather they are *absolute*. The Lord God does not normally change His rules just because one of His creatures thinks they are out of date. I believe that the Ten Commandments are essential for a person to have a healthy, happy, and holy life. These are the standards—the guidelines.

In Ecclesiastes 12:13, when Solomon comes to the conclusion of that magnificent book, he says, "Let us hear the conclusion of the whole matter: Fear God, and keep his commandments: for this is the whole duty of man." In the *King James Version* the word *duty* is in italics, which means it was added by the translators. If you take it away you would better understand the scripture: "Fear God, keep his commandments for this is the whole of man." In other words, this is the kind of life that is lived if a person is whole. This is what it means to be whole.

James 2:10 talks about the whole law. Ecclesiastes 12:13 speaks of the whole man. Here is God's prescription for a life that is holy, happy, and healthy.

When you look at these Ten Commandments you will immediately notice that they are grouped into two major divisions. The first four are Godward. They have to do with our relationship with Him. The next six are manward. They have to do with our relationships to one another. Once they asked the Lord Jesus what was the greatest commandment of all. Jesus stated that the greatest commandment is this: "Thou shalt love the Lord thy God with all thy heart, and with all thy soul, and with all thy mind. The second is like unto it, Thou shalt love thy neighbor as thyself" (Matt. 22:37,39). Jesus grouped the Ten Commandments into two main sections. Number one—love God with everything you have— Godward commandments. Number two—love your neighbor as yourself—manward commandments. The first four have to do with our relationship to God. Number one talks about the unity of God: "no other gods before me." Number two deals with the spirituality of God. Do not "make unto thee any graven images." Number three treats the Deity of God. Do not take My "name . . . in vain."

Number four touches on the sanctity of God. "Remember the sabbath day, to keep it holy."

First we will focus our attention upon God. Isn't it interesting that in the Ten Commandments, God's guidelines for living, that we begin with God? That's where you always begin. The Bible opens like that. "In the beginning God created the heaven and the earth" (Gen. 1:1). Good way to start a world, good way to start a life. "In the beginning God . . . ." Put God first in your life. The Ten Commandments open with a statement of the primacy of God being number one.

I want us to look at this first Commandment—"no other gods before me." In this Commandment there is an assertion. There is also a prohibition and an invitation.

God asserts here His reality. Verse 2—"I am the Lord thy God." The statement assumes the existence and reality of God. Philosophers through the ages have sought to prove the existence of God, but the Bible nowhere tries to prove such. His being and existence are taken for granted. Psalm 14:1 and 53:1 both say: "The fool hath said in his heart, there is no God." A fool is a person who denies a plain fact. So, a person must be the supreme fool who denies the supreme fact. Atheism is not a problem of the head—it's a problem of the heart. "The fool hath said in his heart, there is no God." His head knows better.

This is another verse where some words are in italics. When you take those words out it says: "The fool hath said no God." That fool was basically saying that it is not that God does not exist, but that "I'm not interested in God." That's like you are sitting at a meal and they pass the key lime pie. You say, "no pie." That does not mean the pie does not exist; it means that you do not want any pie at that particular time. There are many people who may not intellectually deny the existence of God, but practically deny His existence because they say, "No God for me. I'm not interested in God. I do not want God intruding into my life." But this very statement assumes the existence of God.

I used to hear the late R. G. Lee, that peerless preacher from Memphis, stress that belief in God is the fundamental postulate of all rational thinking. That is exactly true. You cannot even think straight if you do not believe in the existence of God. It is not the existence of God that is in discussion here. God is rather talking about His unity. He is saying, "I am the Lord thy God, . . . no other gods before me." He is asserting the fact that God is one God. Deuteronomy 6:4 says, "The Lord our God is one Lord."

Israel had just exited the land of Egypt. They had seen the Lord God demolish the false gods of Egypt. Egypt looked like Baghdad in 1991 after God finished with the false gods of Egypt. Now God asserts His sole existence. God is not plural. God is one. "The Lord our God is one Lord." God was teaching that He is not the chairman of the board of gods. He is the *only* God there is. There is one God. What kind of God is this one God?

He tells us in Exodus 20:2 that He is the God of creation. "I am the Lord thy God." The word Lord there is the word, *Jehovah*. Jehovah is God's specific name. It points to His works. It reminds us that He is the God who was, the God who is, the God who ever shall be. He is Jehovah God. Moses was on the same mountain in those wilderness years. When God revealed Himself to Moses out of the burning bush and Moses asked who to tell the people had sent him. He said to tell them "I AM hath sent [thee]" (Ex. 3:14) Jehovah hath sent thee—the God who was, the God who is, and the God who ever shall be.

In the New Testament understanding of that, Jehovah God has revealed Himself in the person of His Son, the Lord Jesus Christ. The Bible says in Colossians 1:15 that Jesus Christ "is the image of the invisible God." Hebrew 1:3 says he is the "express image of his person." John 1:18 says that "No man hath seen God at anytime; the only begotten Son, which is in the bosom of the Father, he hath declared him." When the Old Testament asserts the reality of God—I am Jehovah—you and I as New Testament believers realize that we are referring to none other than our Savior, the Lord Jesus Christ Himself.

In John's Gospel He took that same "I AM" title and applied it to Himself. "Before Abraham was, I am" (8:58). "I am the way, the truth, and the life" (14:6). "I am the bread of life" (6:35). "I am the light of the world" (8:12). "I am the resurrection, and the life" (11:25). And in Revelation, see 1:8; 21:16; 22:13: "I am Alpha and Omega." That's the God we are talking about. He is the God who is Jehovah. But He is also God. "I am the Lord thy God." The word is *Elohim*, which refers specifically to His creative activity. He is *Elohim* the God who brought this universe into existence. Here is a statement that God is the God who created everything there is. I think about the vastness of our creation. Yet, the Bible tells us that the Lord God made it all. I think about the minuteness of our creation. Looking into a microscope you see smaller and smaller worlds unfold before your gaze. I remember that the Lord God made all of this and has given us these Commandments. He is the Lord God of creation.

Not only is He the Lord of creation, He's the Lord of redemption. He says, "I have brought thee out of the land of Egypt, out of the house of bondage." They had crossed over the Red Sea. They were not in the Sinai Peninsula. They had been redeemed by the blood of a substitutionary lamb. They had been led by miraculous power through the Red Sea on dry ground. God said, "Don't ever forget I am the God of redemption." In New Testament terminology Jesus Christ is our Redeemer. John 8:36 says, "If the Son therefore shall make you free, ye shall be free indeed." Isn't it spectacular to know that we are redeemed in the Lord Jesus Christ? The living God is Creator; He is the loving God, and He is the Savior. He is Jesus Christ, our Lord. So, this Commandment sets before us the reality of God. There is an *assertion*.

There is also a *prohibition*. In this First Commandment we also see the rivals to God. In verse 3 He says "Thou shalt have no other gods before me." It is not atheism which is in question but polytheism. He is not battling atheism—there is no God; the question raised in this Commandment is, How many gods are there? God says "I am the Lord thy God, . . . no other gods before me." He is simply saying, "I will have no rivals. I am the only God there is." Just think about this statement for a moment. "No other gods before me." Think, first of all, about the unimaginable possibility that people would place other gods before the only God who is real. Is that possible? Of course it is.

Israel had just come out of polytheistic Egypt, and they were on their way into polytheistic Canaan when God said to them, "Thou shalt have no other gods before me." God had scarcely spoken the Commandment when the children of Israel violated it. They made a golden calf and said, "These be thy gods [plural], O Israel, which brought thee out of the land of Egypt" (Ex. 32:4). What an amazing idea: people would worship false gods—substitute gods—in the place of the real God, the Lord God Jehovah.

Yet that's what you read all through the Old Testament. You will find that the children of Israel seemed to be addicted to polytheism. They worshiped the gods of the peoples around them. There was Baal-Peor, the god of corruption. There was Baal-Zebub (lord of the flies). There was Molech, the fire god. The Israelites even stooped to offering their own sons and daughters in the flames of Molech. How pagan, you say, how uncivilized that people would be guilty of polytheism! Yet, old gods never die. They simply come back in new clothing. We are living in an America where people are still worshiping other gods beside the Lord God. Could Christians even be guilty of that?

The Bible cautions us to beware of "covetousness which is idolatry." The Bible warns of people who become covetous for material things, who become money-conscious, and put money before the worship of God. There are many people who bow the knee before the "almighty dollar." The eagle on a dollar bill can be a vulture that will eat the heart out of some precious soul, or it can become a mockingbird that will make music in some precious soul. When people put money first, they make a god out of it.

The Bible tells us people can make a god out of pleasure. Second Timothy 3:4 says that people become "lovers of pleasure more than lovers of God." Who comes first in your time? Do you think in America we have become so sports-mad and so amusement-crazed that we put these kinds of things before the worship of the Lord God?

Of course, sex has been made a god. You can hardly pick up a modern novel without finding a preoccupation with sex. You can barely turn on the television without seeing the preoccupation with sex by means of advertisements and movies. Hollywood has become the prophet of the goddess of sex in America. Many American people have become Peeping Toms in their own dens because of television. Do you think we have made a god out of sex?

Do you think we have made a god out of education? It's wonderful to get an education. But education is a means to an end; it is not an end unto itself.

Do you think people make a god out of themselves? It's so real that people put other gods before the true God.

Not only is there the *unimaginable possibility,* but look at the *unnatural infidelity* of it. God says, "Don't have any other gods before Me." Loyalty to a false god, a substitute god, involves disloyalty to the true God. You can't be loyal to both at the same time. Jesus made it plain, "No man can serve two masters." It is like going east or going west. You cannot go west while you are going east. You cannot travel east while you are going west. You are either going east or west—you can't go both ways at the same time. The same is true about God. You cannot be faithful to the true God and be faithful to a false god at the same time. *Unnatural infidelity*. For people to try to hold onto the true God, and be loyal to Him, yet be faithful to their own false god at the same time, is like a man who has a lover that he brings into his own house to live with his wife and children. How unnatural. How unfaithful. Yet, that's what people do when they worship another god.

Now, see the *unquestionable futility* of it. "Thou shalt have no other gods before me." We could translate that "in the place of Me." That would mean a substitute god. It could mean "alongside Me"—an additional god. The Lord affirms that when you put any other god between you and Him, it will usher futility into your life. There is a statement in the Psalms which contends that you become like the god you worship. That is true. Your morals will reflect the kind of god you worship. You look at the gods America is worshiping, and you find that our people are becoming exactly like the gods they are worshiping. If you are polytheistic in your worship, you will be polytheistic in your personality. The Bible calls it idolatry. Psychology calls it neurosis. When people begin to worship many gods, and have many loyalties in their lives instead of that one, central loyalty to the true Lord, it causes disintegration of human personality. So there is a prohibition here against the rivals of God.

There is also an *invitation* here—the reverence for God. "Thou shalt have no other gods before me." It is certainly implied in this Commandment that if you are willing to have no other gods, you can have God. If you will put other gods out of your life, God says, "I'll show up." The tremendous invitation in this command of God is to give reverence to Him, to give reverence to the God who is real—the God who will brook no rivals. This statement means that you and I can know God personally. That's one of the most astounding concepts ever to grip the human heart—that we can know God personally. Think of it—the great God of creation condescends to reveal Himself to you and to me. Job inquired, "Canst thou by searching find out God?" (Job 11:7). The answer is no.

Jesus said in Matthew 11:25, "I thank thee, O Father, Lord of heaven and earth, because thou hast hid these things from the wise and prudent, and hast revealed them unto babes." You cannot find God by your own intellect, by your own reasoning processes, but if you want to know God you can know God personally. He will reveal Himself personally to you. In John 17:3 Jesus averred, "And this is life eternal, that they may know thee the only true God, and Jesus Christ whom thou hast sent."

Paul spoke to a group on one of his missionary journeys in Acts 14:15 "to turn from these vanities unto the living God." He said to the believers in Thessalonica "how ye turned to God from idols, to serve the living and the true God" (1 Thess. 1:9). If you want to know God you can meet Him intimately. You can know Him initially in the salvation experience. You can know Him increasingly as you grow in grace and in the knowledge of the Lord. You can know Him infinitely. You can enjoy the presence and knowledge of God throughout eternity.

When Jesus was being tested of the devil who tempted Jesus to fall down and worship him, Jesus replied, "Get thee hence Satan: for it is written, Thou shalt worship the Lord thy God, and him only shalt thou serve" (Matt. 4:10). You can love God supremely—God and God alone. Make Him absolutely number one. Make Him first in your life. You can love Him supremely.

You can worship Him humbly. There is no greater privilege given to a human being than that of bowing before the great God of this universe and removing from one's heart and life any other competing idol, any rival gods, and worship God and God alone.

Look at verse 2—the Lord says, "I am the Lord thy God." He is simply saying, "I can be real personally to you." It's not enough to affirm there is a God. It's not enough for you to say, "He is the God." You need to be able to say, "He is *my* God. "The Lord is my shepherd; I shall not want" (Ps. 23:1). Can you say that? Can you say Jesus is *my* Savior? He is *my* Lord. He is *my* God.

I think about Thomas. There is so much of Thomas in all of us. After the Lord Jesus Christ was raised from the dead, Thomas said, "I won't believe it until I put my hand in the nail prints, until I thrust my hand into his side." So, the Lord Jesus Christ revealed

Himself in His resurrection glory to the disciples on that Sunday night. He challenged, "OK, Thomas, put your fingers in the nail prints. Put your hand in My side" (John 21:26–27, author). Thomas stood before the living Lord Jesus and then fell down, crying, "My Lord and my God" (v. 28) Can you say that? You cannot believe in someone, you cannot call on someone to save you in whom you have not believed. You can't believe in someone of whom you have not heard. You can't unless God sends a preacher.

The tenth chapter in the Book of Romans exactly explains what God is doing. God has sent the preacher. The preacher has preached God's Word. You have heard God's Word. Will you believe it? Will you believe that this God is knowable, lovable, worthy of our worship? "Whosoever shall call upon the name of the Lord shall be saved" (v. 10). If you will call on Him, you will come to know this God personally.

2
How Big Is Your God?

(vv. 4–6)

Several years ago I read a book by J. B. Phillips (who also has a translation of the New Testament) entitled *Your God Is Too Small*. It was an intriguing book because he basically wrote that many people have a concept of God that belittles Him. The reason the Ten Commandments begin with our relationship with God is because we must be sure that our relationship is right with Him before we can expect our relationship with others to be what it ought to be.

The first four Commandments are Godward. They have to do with our relationship to God. The first two Commandments hang together. The First Commandment tells us who God is. Commandment two tells us how we are to worship God. The First Commandment teaches us that we are to worship the right God. The second says that we are not to worship the right God in the wrong way. The impulse to worship is universal. Anywhere you go, among any tribe or race of people, you will find those people engaged in worship of some kind. It is a God-given inclination. There is a God consciousness in the heart of every human being. Atheism is unnatural to the heart of mankind. God has placed that God-consciousness in us so it is unnatural to be an atheist. Atheism is as unnatural to the human heart as singing is to a Georgia mule. It is absolutely out of place.

So, when a person becomes an atheist, he really commits moral suicide. He violates his own inner awareness of God and in so doing he cuts himself off from the source of morality. This Commandment has to do with this matter of how we are to worship God. How big a God do we worship? I will try to squeeze all I can out of this Commandment. I believe it is extremely important that we understand how to worship God and we understand how big our God is.

Prohibited

Let's look at the Second Commandment and note what is prohibited. This Commandment prohibits basically two things. In verse 4 we are not to make any graven image or any likeness of God, and we are not to bow down to them or serve them. That's what God prohibits. When we read that statement it calls to mind a variety of thoughts. Certain people have the idea that this forbids the use of art in any form. Some feel there aren't to be any pictures around a church. There are to be no forms of art. Some even go so far as to argue that there is to be no music because music is an art form.

If that were the interpretation, then God Himself has violated the Commandment later in this very book. In the magnificent tabernacle there were cherubim and all kinds of gorgeous colors. There were altars and pieces of furniture that were beautifully and lavishly made. All of that taught lessons about the God we worship. So, He is not teaching that there is to be no art or that art is not a legitimate form to use as an instructive method. God declares that art which is intended to be an *object* of worship *is* prohibited. He has in mind graven images, idols, and statues made for worship. There has always been a human tendency to do exactly what this Commandment says we are not to do.

In Romans 1:23 Paul lays out the sinfulness of the human race: "They have changed the glory of the uncorruptible God into an image made like to corruptible man, and to birds and fourfooted beasts, and creeping things." Then verse 25 states, "Who changed the truth of God into a lie, and worshiped and served the creature more than the Creator." So, mankind has had a tendency to do this all along—to make a god. Man has bowed down before creeping creatures, before images of dogs and frogs and crocodiles and snakes and all kinds of beings.

The children of Israel had that bent. We won't even leave the Book of Exodus until the people will have a golden calf made and cry out, "These be thy gods, O Israel, which brought thee up out of the land of Egypt" (32:4). All through the history of the children of

Israel you will find that they had a constant problem violating this very Commandment. Jeroboam set up golden calves in Dan and also in Beersheba. Even the brazen serpent that was used in the wilderness to deliver them from snakebites was later made a graven object of worship on the part of the Israelites. Only when Israel was carried into captivity were they cured of the problem of idolatry.

That instinct is there. That tendency for man to make graven images and mold his own gods is constantly there. The Bible prophesies that, at the end of the age, idolatry is exactly the kind of worship many people are going to prefer. In Revelation 13 we are told about the Antichrist. It is predicted that there will be an image of the Antichrist made and set up in the temple at Jerusalem. The Antichrist will require that the whole world bow down and worship his image.

This proclivity thrives in our day. We find the use of statues and idols as aids to worship. Perhaps you have visited some of the massive cathedrals in Europe. In Italy several years ago I was in a magnificent cathedral. There was a statue of Simon Peter there. I watched the people as they stood in long lines. When they would reach the statue, they would kiss the toes of the statue. So many people had done so that the toes of the statue were absolutely wiped out.

Some argue, "I use these kinds of things, but I don't really worship them. They are just really aids to worship." I'm not too sure about that. Suppose one of you ladies walks into a restaurant and catches your husband passionately embracing another woman. He sees you out of the corner of his eye and protests, "Wait a minute, I know what you're thinking. I want you to know this is not what is appears to be. When I saw this woman she had an amazing resemblance to you. She just looked so much like you that I simply couldn't resist. But I want you to know that when I'm hugging her, I'm hugging you. When I'm kissing her, I'm really loving you."

I have no idea how far some of you guys would go with that line, but I wouldn't make it halfway to first base. The Bible emphasizes that you are not to make graven images, and you are not to bow down and worship them. Why is this prohibited? There are two reasons God prohibits the making of graven images.

Number one—it distorts God. If you are going to worship God correctly, then you must have a correct conception of God. That's why it's important to know how big your God is. The size of your God, the concept of your God, will determine how you worship that God. Jesus, in John 4:24, said, "God is a Spirit: and they that worship him must worship him in spirit and in truth." It is impossible for a material image to represent a spiritual God. God can hear; images cannot. God can feel—images cannot. God can help—images cannot. Any attempt to represent God distorts Him and is a poor imitation.

I heard about a girl busily drawing at school. The teacher came over and asked, "Honey, what are you doing?" She replied, "Oh, I'm drawing a picture of God."

The teacher smiled and answered, "Sugar, nobody knows what God looks like."

The girl said, "They will when I get through!" That's a cute story, but you and I recognize there is no adequate means of representing who God is by any physical form—any attempt to represent Him. In fact, the Bible presents the attempts to do so as utter foolishness. In Isaiah 44, Isaiah, with sarcastic language, refers to a blacksmith who "fires up" a god. Then he speaks of the carpenter who "nails up" a god. Then he writes of a cook who goes into the kitchen and tries to "cook up" a god. He is basically writing that you cannot make anything that will represent the God who is worthy of your worship.

An image is fixed, unchanging. As you and I grow in our understanding of the Lord, our concept of God should expand and mature. I am not sure about you, but my God is bigger in my understanding than He was years ago. I have grown in my concept. When you make a graven image of God, you fix God. An image is limited. God is unlimited. An image is local. God is universal. An image is temporal. God is eternal. An image is material. God is spiritual. When you make a graven image, it distorts God.

When you bow down before an idol, it not only distorts God, it degrades Him. To bring God down to the level of man or to that of bugs, frogs, dogs, beasts, or fish—how that degrades God!

How would you feel if you were God and people made images of your creation and worshiped them? Most of us don't like to have a poor picture made of us. Have you ever had someone make an embarrassing photo of you and show it to everybody? Maybe one of your baby pictures when you were a fat little kid? That's embarrassing. Nobody likes a poor representation of oneself. In fact, most of us want a photographer to make it look better than we deserve. I like the motto of the photographer who said, "Where there is beauty I take it; where there is none I make it."

The Bible says that we are not to make unto ourselves any graven image. It distorts and degrades God.

In this Commandment there is first of all something *prohibited*. If you look carefully at this Commandment you see that there is something . . .

Protected

Verse 5 says, "For I the Lord thy God am a jealous God." Isn't that an amazing statement about God? Exodus 34:14 says, "For thou shalt worship no other god: for the Lord, whose name is Jealous, is a jealous God." We don't normally put those two together. That doesn't sound right. When we employ the word *jealous*, we normally use it in a negative sense. When you dig into the root meaning of that word *jealous* there is heat there. It means to be inflamed. It is akin to the word *zeal*, "on fire." Jealousy is a zeal to protect a relationship.

The Bible teaches that when you come to know the Lord you enter into a covenant relationship with Him, which is compared to marriage. In the Old Testament, Israel was called the "bride" of Jehovah. In the New Testament, believers are called the "bride" of Christ. We are in a spiritual marriage relationship.

The Bible uses anthropomorphic imagery—related to mankind. The Bible attempts to help us understand God by using terms that relate to man in relationship to God. The Bible talks, for instance, about the "hands" of God, the "eyes" of God. Those are anthropomorphic terms. When God says I am "a jealous God," He is trying to communicate a relationship we have to Him that is extra special to Him and which He is going to protect. God is saying, "You belong to Me. You are special to Me, and I'm going to fight to maintain that relationship."

I heard my friend, Adrian Rogers, make a statement which is quite illustrative. No athlete has a right to be jealous of any other athlete. Young athlete, you do not own athletics. No singer has a right to be jealous of any other singer. No one singer owns music.

But a husband has a right to be jealous of his wife. I'm not talking about that in the bad sense. Not a suspicious, destructive, detrimental kind of jealousy—that's not what I'm talking about. I'm using *jealous* in a good sense. A husband has a right to be jealous of his wife because she is his wife. She doesn't belong to anybody else in the world but to him. A wife has a right to be jealous of her husband because he is her spouse. He belongs to her and no one else in the whole world.

God is saying, "I'm the only God there is. I am your God, you belong to Me. I am jealous of that relationship." He is protecting that which is very percious. He is jealous to maintain that relationship. He is saying, "I'm expecting from you your total life." When you marry you are to share the life of that mate. You have intimacies together. God wants your total life, not merely what you do on Sunday but every day. We tend to divide aspects of life into the spiritual and the secular—but in the eyes of God it is all spiritual. He wants all of our life every day of our life. He wants to have our undivided attention and time.

He also wants our complete love. The Lord has given Himself to us with an everlasting love (see Jer. 33:3). He loves us wholeheartedly. He loves us infinitely. God is saying, "I want your total love. I don't want anybody to come between Me and you." Idolatry is putting anything between you and God. When anything or anyone comes between you and God, that is idolatry.

Augustine observed that idolatry is worshiping anything that ought to be used and using anything that ought to be worshiped. God is simply saying, "I love you; I want all of your love." There are different kinds of idols and images besides those of wood and stone. Think about how people love their houses before the Lord, how people love cars, how people love clothes, how people love material things. Yet, the Lord demands your total love.

Total life, total love, total loyalty. He is saying, "I want you to be totally loyal to Me. I want to be absolutely first in your life." In this commandment there is something protected. God says, "I am a jealous God; I have a zeal to protect our relationship."

Let's dig somewhat deeper. This becomes fascinating. Not only *prohibited*—no other gods, no images of God. *Something protected*—I the Lord thy God am a jealous God. But there is also in this commandment something

Projected

He projects something in the future. He says ". . . visiting the iniquity of the fathers upon the children until the third and fourth generation of them that hate me; And showing mercy unto the thousands of them that love me, and keep my commandments" (vv. 5–6). God demands that we be exceedingly careful to observe this Commandment, because the way we worship God projects something on our children and our grandchildren. The way we worship God is no minor matter.

First of all God talks about a visitation of misery. "Visiting iniquities of the fathers on the children unto the third and fourth generation." When we first read this we contend, "That's not fair! Why should a helpless little child be held guilty for something the parents did?" He didn't claim they would be guilty, but that he would visit iniquity. He is pointing out that the children sometimes pay an awful price because of the sins of their parents. Isn't that true?

Some of you were brought up in the home of an alcoholic. All of the days of your life you will bear the scars of that situation. The sin of your father or mother's drinking has reaped untold misery, agony, and heartache in your own life. Romans 5:12 says, "Wherefore, as by one man sin entered into the world, and so death passed upon all men, for that all have sinned." In the fall of Adam we all picked up the baggage. God is saying that we inherited the fallen estate of Adam.

It's like a son whose father left him a farm for an inheritance. The farm was rundown, covered with thorns, briars, and weeds, and the ground was eroding. He inherited it from his father, but it was a wretched farm. That is exactly what we have all inherited from father Adam, and from our own fathers we have reaped the results and the impact of their sin.

It's true in the realm of physical health. You go to the doctor for an examination, and the doctor will start asking you about your parents. "Does your dad have any history of heart disease?" "Is there any cancer in your family?" He understands that in our genes are the seeds of all the diseases that plague this human race. They continue from one generation to another.

See a psychologist, and he starts talking with you and asking questions about your parents and grandparents. It has all come down—visiting the iniquities on the children to the third and fourth generations. That is involved here, but, thank you, there is far more. God stresses that how you served and worship Him will have an impact on your children and your grandchildren as to how they respond to God.

I want to share what I feel is the most vivid illustration of that truth I have ever read anywhere. In 2 Chronicles 26:16 we read the account of King Uzziah, a godly man. Read his record, and we learn in the opening verses that he was indeed a good man. "But when he was strong, his heart was lifted up to his destruction: for he transgressed against the Lord His God, and went into the temple of the Lord to burn incense upon the altar of incense." That was not his prerogative. Back in those days they had priests who did that. This was not a New Testament situation. You weren't supposed to worship God in that manner. You went through a priest. I guess Uzziah thought, *Wait a minute; every man worships God according to the dictates of his own heart.*

Ever heard that? No! You don't worship according to the dictates of your own heart—you worship according to the dictates of God's Word. He transgressed against the Lord by going into the temple. In verse 18 the priest said: "It appertaineth not unto thee, Uzziah, to burn incense unto the Lord, but to the priests." Then look at verse 19, "Then Uzziah was wroth [got mad at the preacher]." Verse 21 says he contracted leprosy and was cut off from the house of the Lord. Here was a good man, but he created a severe problem because he tried to worship God in the wrong way and had trouble at church. That was one man and his sin. That was King Uzziah,

a father, and his sin. So far that's the only effect you can see.
Read on.

In chapter 27 you can read about his son, Jotham, twenty-five
years old when he began to reign. He was a good boy, too. Remember he was the son of a father who had trouble at church. Note
verse 2. "He did that which was right in the sight of the Lord,
according to all that his father Uzziah did; howbeit he entered not
into the temple of the Lord." He was a good boy, but he quit going
to church. Why? Dad had trouble at church, a problem, a church
fuss. So, Jotham entered not into the house of the Lord. That was
not the end of it. There was a father, and the iniquities of the father
were being visited upon the son.

Move on to chapter 28.

> Ahaz [grandson of Uzziah] was twenty years old when he began to
> reign, and he reigned sixteen years in Jerusalem: but he did not
> that which was right in the sight of the Lord, like David his father:
> For he walked in the ways of the kings of Israel, and made also
> molten images for Baalim. Moreover he burnt incense in the valley
> of the son of Hinnom, and burnt his children in the fire (vv. 1–3).

He became such a devout worshiper of images to the extent that
he took his own boys and girls and threw them into the fire. Verse
24 says, "And Ahaz gathered together the vessels of the house of
God, and cut in pieces the vessels of the house of God, and shut up
the doors of the house of the Lord." Get the picture? The father
started worshiping God the wrong way and had trouble. His son
quit going altogether. The grandson became a devil worshiper,
sacrificing his own children, and he shut the doors of the house of
the Lord.

Some of you are in danger of visiting your iniquities on your own
children and your grandchildren by the way you worship God and
by your whole attitude toward God. You have a gripe, and you
start fussing and fighting, and you have children who are listening
to every bit of it. Or a Sunday night comes, and you say, "There's a
ball game tonight; I'll just stay home." Your son is sitting there, and
he may not consciously think you are saying to him that the
worship of God is not nearly as important as the ball game. The
way you worship God is serious business. Your attitudes and
words are making indelible impressions on your kids. One of these

days, if you aren't most careful, and if you don't change how you are going about it, you are going to have spiritual problems with your own family.

One of my preacher friends told me this story. He had a church where one of the men was very unkind toward and critical of the pastor. This man's boy landed in jail. He asked the preacher to visit the boy in jail. So, the preacher did. When the preacher reached the jail, the boy asked with a snarl, "What are *you* doing here?"

The preacher answered, "Your dad asked me to come over here and talk with you about the Lord."

The boy came back, "The Lord! Man, the way my daddy has talked about you, made fun of the church, laughed about the church, and criticized the church! I don't want to hear anything out of you. Just go on your way. I'm not interested in anything you have to say." It's very serious how you worship God.

The Scripture states God visited the iniquities upon the children and the grandchildren to the third and fourth generations. But notice a demonstration of mercy.

Verse 6: "And showing mercy unto thousands of them that love me." Notice the contrast—three and four thousands. There is only one movement that can stop that downward spiral of sin and incorrect worship, and it is that upward spiral of God's mercy and grace. Romans 5:20 says, "Where sin abounded, grace did much more abound." That's why we must send missionaries to foreign countries. These poor people bow down before their idols because idolatry has been passed from generation to generation. All that can stop the downward trend is the uprising of mercy, love, and grace found in worship of the true God. God will bless you if you will live for Him, worship Him, serve Him, honor Him, and be true to Him. God will bless you on down the road with your children.

I do not make many references to my family in the pulpit—not that I don't love my family. I love them dearly, but I realize you love yours, too. I hope you will excuse this one reference. I do have a granddaughter, and she is the prettiest girl in all the world. One night this week she called (going on four now), and her mother has taught her to sing "Amazing Grace." She's not timid. She said, "Poppie, I want to sing 'Amazing Grace' for you." She sang it at the top of her voice; from "Amazing" to "I once . . . was blind, but now I see." I thought it was marvelous. Finest rendition of "Amazing Grace" which has ever been sung on earth! The child probably needs to sign a recording contract.

But when I hung up that phone, tears gushed from my eyes. I was so thankful that I know Jesus, but I am far from perfect. My children will testify to that. But they do know I'm real. They are aware I've tried to live Jesus in front of them. I exulted, "Oh, Lord, I'm so thankful my daughter loves Jesus. Now, she is teaching my granddaughter to love Him." "Showing mercy unto the thousands of them that love me, and keep my commandments" (Ex. 20:6). Jesus said the father "seeketh such to worship him." The negative side of the Commandment is: don't worship any graven images. The positive side is: worship Me.

The word *worship* is made up of two words—*worth* and *ship*. *Th* dropped out, and it became worship. When you worship you declare the worth of God. You are emphasizing how wonderful God is. That's why in the Book of Revelation, when the Lamb is seated upon the throne, the congregated redeemed in heaven sing "Worthy is the Lamb that was slain to receive power, and honor, and glory . . ." (Rev. 5:12). He alone is worthy. That's why our Savior said, "Thou shalt worship the Lord thy God, and him only shalt thou serve" (Matt. 4:10). Did you notice that worship always comes before service? Worship— and then service.

Do you remember Mary and Martha? Martha became all hot and bothered with the pots and the pans in the kitchen. She came running in trying to tell Jesus what to do. She called him Lord, then proceeded to tell Him what to do. "Why don't you get Mary in here to help me, Lord?" (Luke 10:40, author). He said, "Martha, Martha, thou art careful and troubled about many things. But Mary hath chosen that good part. But one thing is needful: . . . " and (vv. 41–42a). He was saying, "Martha, far more than anything you do for Me is just having you with Me. I'm far more interested in your worshiping Me than in your serving Me because you can't serve Me the way you ought to serve Me until you are worshiping Me the way you ought to worship Me."

God commands us not to make any graven images because He has already revealed Himself in an image. Colossians 1:15 says that the Lord Jesus "is the image of the invisible God." Hebrews 1:3

says that Jesus Christ "is the express image of his person." Jesus said "he that hath seen me hath seen the Father" (John 14:9). The only representation we need of God is the revelation He has given to us in the person of His own Son, the Lord Jesus Christ. If you want to know God, meet Him in the person of His Son Jesus.

Wouldn't you like to know that Jesus?

3
Be Careful With God's Name

(v. 7)

Two of the Ten Commandments have to do with sins of speech. This Commandment—"Thou shalt not take God's name in vain" (v. 7); and the Ninth Commandment—"Thou shalt not bear false witness against thy neighbor" (v. 16) One of God's most beautiful gifts to mankind is speech. Among many things this is one that distinguishes people from animals. God has given man the ability to express himself in marvelous, unusual ways. Isn't it a tragedy that mankind would take the beautiful gift of speech and misuse it? To misuse that gift, for instance, to curse persons. In James 3:9 the Bible says, "therewith [the tongue] curse we men." What a sad thing that people would take the gift of speech and use it to curse people. An even sadder thing it is for someone to take God's gracious gift of language and use the gift that God has given him as a means of abusing and misusing the name of God Himself.

Our Lord Jesus, in the Model Prayer, taught us to pray: "Our Father which art in haven, hallowed be thy name" (Matt. 6:9). May Your name be honored.

Let us focus on this Commandment—"Thou shalt not take the name of the Lord thy God in vain."

The *Definition* of God's Name

In the Bible names were often used for particular reasons. A name sometimes would identify character. There was a man in the Bible named Nabal. His name means foolish and Nabal was a foolish man indeed. Sometimes parents would give names to their children as expressions of hope and adoration. By the giving of that name they would express a great ambition for that child.

Sometimes a name would be given in the midst of certain circumstances. When Benjamin was born, his father, Jacob, named him
Benjamin which meant "the son of my right hand." So, names
speak of character and reputation.

The name of God always had to be revealed. We can never
comprehend God by our own reason. But God has to reveal Himself to us. In the revelation of God's name we have first of all a
definition of His character. The name of God tells us what kind of
God He is. The name of God tells us what His character is. The
Bible has a great deal to say about the name of God. I have written
down several verses about the name of God.

Psalm 8:1 says—"How excellent is thy name in all the earth!"
In Psalm 20:5 we read—"in the name of our God we will set
up our banners." In Psalm 111:9—"holy and reverend is his
name." Proverbs 18:10 says, "the name of the Lord is a strong
tower."

So, the name of God is profoundly sacred. The orthodox Jews
would not use the name of God. They would not pronounce the
name of God. In fact, when the scribes were making copies of the
Holy Scripture, when they came to the name of God they would
place their pen down, rise, go bathe themselves, and put on
different garments. Then they would come with a pen that had
never been used before and with a brand new pen they would
write down the holy name of God. That's what the name repre-
sents. It is a revelation of the holy, sacred character of God.
What an awful thought it is that someone would drag that
name down into the mud. It is a revelation of the character of
God.

It is also a revelation of the nature of God. By giving His names in
Scripture, God reveals His nature. He tells us what kind of God He
is. There are over three hundred names for God given to us in the
Bible. Why does the Bible give so many names to God? Because no
one name can adequately convey all that God is. The nature of God
is so wonderful, vast, and tremendous that it takes a multitude of
names to identify His character and His nature to us.

Already in our study in Exodus we've run across several names
for God. There is the name Elohim. In this Commandment the
Lord says [I am the Lord thy God], Thou shalt not take the name of
the Lord thy God in vain." The word, "God," there is the word

Elohim. This is one of the great names for God in the Bible. It means that God is the faithful One. He is the strong One.

The word translated *Lord* is the word *Jehovah.* He is Jehovah God. When Moses was on Mount Sinai previously the Lord revealed Himself there. Moses asked, "What will I tell the people Your name is?" God said, "Tell them I Am hath sent thee. Tell them Jehovah hath sent thee" (see Ex. 3:13–14.). God is the eternal self-existing one. He is the God who was. He is the God who is. He is the God who evermore shall be. He is Jehovah God.

There are some other names that already had been given for God. Exodus 17:15 tells us, "Moses built an altar and called the name of it Jehovah-nissi," which means the Lord is our banner. That is a beautiful unveiling of the nature of God. It tells us that we win the victory in the name of God. That God is the banner and under the banner of God we win our victory.

In Exodus 15:26 there was another name revealed for God. "I am the Lord that healeth thee." The Hebrew word is *rapha.* I am Jehovah-rapha. I am the God who healeth thee.

All through the Bible we have this unfolding of the wonderful nature of God by means of His names. But God gave one final, full revelation of Himself in a name. Matthew 1:21 says that the angel said to Mary and Joseph, "thou shalt call his name Jesus, for he shall save his people from their sins." That is the full and the final revelation of the character and nature of God. God put it all together in the name of Jesus Christ. When God wanted to say it all He revealed Himself as Jesus in the person of His Son. What a name for God! The name of Jesus! Jesus is the veracity of truth. Jesus is the visibility of God. Jesus is the verity of love. Jesus is the victory of grace. That name Jesus is honey to the taste. It is harmony to the heart. It is healing to the soul. It is the name above every name. What a wonderful name! There is just something about that name of Jesus.

When the Lord gives this Commandment He, first of all, wants us to understand the sacredness of His character and His nature, the definition of God's name.

The *Desecration* of God's Name

"Thou shalt not take the name of the Lord thy God in vain." The word, "vain," here means empty of content. It means to make void of meaning. It means to be irreverent. The *New International Version* translates the Commandment this way: "You shall not misuse the name of the Lord your God." *The Living Bible* paraphrases it: "You shall not use the name of Jehovah your God irreverently."

Here is a specific commandment that the name of God is not to be misused or abused. I want to suggest to you the way God's name can be taken in vain. Let me mention some of the ways people misuse God's name—ways they are irreverent toward God's name. One of the obvious ways is by profanity. In that connection I want to go on record that I really am offended by crudity. I don't like for people to use crudity in their language. When people make reference to body parts or body functions in language that's offensive to me, it is crude.

Little children get to a certain stage in their lives when their bodily parts and functions become funny to them. They laugh about it and it's cute to them. We laugh at them because it's cute—they are little children. Most normal people grow intellectually beyond that period of their babyhood. Unfortunately, there are some people who never seem to grow past that stage. Somehow they just kind of fix on that particular stage and that which is so babylike and so trivial and trite, they carry with them all their lives. Crudity becomes a part of their language. Let me encourage you not to use crudity in your language.

Now when I'm talking about profanity I'm talking about something far more serious than that. I am talking about using the name of God in an irreverent, frivolous, and disrespectful way. I remember when the free-speech movement began in this country. It was pretty bad at that time, but that just really accelerated the whole problem. Today we are living in a veritable cesspool of immoral, godless, and indecent language. Yet, the Bible says "Thou shalt not take the name of the Lord thy God in vain."

I feel sorry for our young people in some ways. They are brought up in an atmosphere where profanity is so common. It is so everyday. We are living in a filthy, vulgar, dirty, rotten-talking generation. It is a shame, and it is displeasing to a holy God. I am astounded at the language of ladies today. Sometimes in restaurants and places of business I am amazed at the language of ladies. I hear ladies using words that you used to hear mostly from men, and then only by the most vulgar of them. Profanity is commonly used today. What a tragedy is the use of profanity.

I can't think of anything that is more illustrative of the lack of sense and sensibility than is the use of profanity. That's why it especially offends me when people who have degrees from reputable schools make use of profanity in their language. It really bugs me when graduates of Harvard and Yale and places like that can't use enough vocabulary from their college education to express themselves forcibly without profanity. It's a tragedy that people do that. A lot of people seem like they went to school in hell and the devil was their teacher. A lot of people seem to have a garbage can for a mind. They seem to specialize in new and twisted ways of defiling the holy name of God. It is a pointless thing for person to use profanity.

Alex Dunlap facetiously wrote "ten reasons why I swear":

1. It pleases Mother so much.
2. It is a fine mark of manliness.
3. It proves I have self-control.
4. It indicates how clearly my mind operates.
5. It makes my conversation so pleasing to everybody.
6. It leaves no doubt in anyone's mind as to my good breeding.
7. It impresses people that I have more than an ordinary education.
8. It is an unmistakable sign of culture and refinement.
9. It makes me a very desirable personality among women and children and respectable society.
10. It is my way of honoring God who said "Thou shalt not take the name of the Lord thy God in vain."

It is a senseless, foolish form of speech.

People don't get paid for profanity. So, you work cheap. You lay aside your character as a gentleman, you inflict pain on your family and friends, you break this Commandment, you insult God Almighty, and you do it all for nothing. What a terrible thing profanity is! It shows disrespect for the holy name of God. You are taking that name by which people are saved, that name by which people are healed, that name by which lives are transformed, and you are pulling that holy name down into the muck, mire, and slime. It is showing utter disregard for God's Commandment. God said don't take My name in vain and yet mankind shakes its fist in God's face, sneers in God's face, and blasphemes His holy name out loud for God and the whole world to hear. It shows utter disrespect for other people.

Sometimes people go to a ball game and one crowd starts chanting to the other—"Go to hell, Florida, go to hell, Florida." Another crowd chants—"Go to hell, Florida State, go to hell, Florida State." People think that's cute, funny. Think about that— for one human being to say to another human being "Go to hell." A person who says that has no conception whatsoever of what hell is all about. Jesus said hell is a place where the worm dieth not, where there is weeping and gnashing of teeth, and where the soul is in torment forever and ever. How awful for one human being to tell another to go to a terrible place like that!

How equally terrible for someone to use the name of God to condemn someone to go to a place of destruction. God's last name is not *damn*. Yet, people use that term. The word *damn* is an abbreviation of the word, *damnation*. When people use that kind of profanity they are slurring the character of God. They know absolutely nothing whatsoever about God. God never consigned any human being to go to hell. God has never been responsible for condemning anybody to the damnation of hell. When a man goes to hell he goes there by his own choice. When a man is condemned in eternal damnation he commits moral suicide. He does it on his own. What an awful thing to smear the character of God and to call upon God to do that which He has never done—to condemn a human soul to hell.

I believe this Commandment not only includes that, I believe it includes secondhand swearing. You say, "Preacher, I don't mean anything by it, it's just an innocent habit." I do believe there are lost people whose profanity is so common to their conversation they don't even know they are doing it. Lost people who don't have the blessed Holy Spirit within them never are even aware of what they are saying. It is a serious thing, though. God said don't do it. You say, "Preacher, I just cuss a little bit." That's like somebody saying I just kill a little bit. Or, I just commit adultery a little bit.

Then, there is secondhand cussing. Take the word *damn*. *Darn* is an abbreviation of the word *damn*. Other words people use are *gosh*, which is a euphemism for God; *golly* is also a euphemism for

God; *gee* is a euphemism for Jesus. I know some of you who use those words and you don't really mean that. You didn't even know what you were doing. Now you know. Some people would be stunned at what they were saying when they say words like *golly, gosh, darn.* Yet the Bible says "Thou shalt not take the name of the Lord thy God in vain." It's an awful sin.

When a nation starts being vulgar and filthy in its language it just lowers the overall moral level of that society. America is in bad, bad shape. You can hardly turn on a television program and not hear it. You can scarcely read a piece of literature and not read it. You have to wade through scum to read most of the literature that's being written today in the name of realism. It's a sin against a holy God.

This business of undue frivolity or undue familiarity with the things of God takes His name in vain, too. Ephesians 5:4 says— "Neither filthiness, nor foolish talking, nor jesting which are not convenient: but rather giving of thanks." That's talking about joking in the name of God; being frivolous with the name of God. There is a place for humor. "A merry heart doeth good like a medicine" (Prov. 17:22). I thank God for laughter. I enjoy life. There are two ways to go through life. You can go through life miserable or you can go through life happy. I choose to go through life happy. I use humor in preaching. Humor is an effective device in preaching. Sometimes it gets the truth across. Someone asked Charles Spurgeon about humor one time. He said, "I use humor. I tickle my oyster with humor until its shell is open—then I put the knife in."

That is certainly true. Humor can be an effective device of getting across what you are wanting to say. But there is never a place for taking the holy, sacred things of God and putting them down in the gutter and being light and irreverent about the holy things of God. We break this Commandment by our profanity.

Ask God to clean your speech. Ask God to give you the right kind of words to say. When people get saved they lose about half their vocabulary. Ask God to help you learn the language of Zion. Instead of saying a cuss word, say *hallelulah.* Instead of using profanity, say *praise the Lord.* Instead of using some of those words, say *amen, glory to God.* They will think you are nuts, but that's all right. You go ahead and do it and you'll not be breaking this Commandment.

I think we violate this Commandment not only by profanity but by dishonesty. The Lord in Matthew 5:33–36 talked about swearing. He said not to swear at all. Leviticus 19:12 says, "Ye shall not swear by my name falsely, neither shalt thou profane the name of thy God." I don't think that forbids the taking of oaths in a court of law, but I think it forbids attaching the name of God to your dishonest, untruthful statements. When a person is constantly having to call on God to avow the truthfulness of what he is saying, it sometimes creates a doubt in one's mind as to whether or not that person is indeed telling the truth. Sometimes people are saying "in the name of God, this is true," and you are wondering all along if this is really true. Matthew 5:37 says for the believer to "let your speech be Yea, yea, Nay, nay." Let your word be your bond. Don't tack God's name onto your dishonesty by violating this Commandment.

Another way we violate this Commandment is by insincerity. Jesus talked about some who would make false professions. In Matthew 7 the Lord said, "many will say to me in that day, Lord, Lord, have we not prophesied in thy name? and in thy name have cast out devils? and in thy name done wonderful works?" Then the Lord said, "I never knew you: depart from me" (vv. 21–22). When we profess that which we do not possess, when we claim an experience with Christ which is not real in our life we are taking the name of the Lord in vain. It is false profession. False praying— in Matthew 6 the Lord says, "When ye pray, use not vain repetitions, as the heathen do: for they think they shall be heard for their much speaking" (v. 7). We do not say prayers. We pray prayers. When we say prayers insincerely we are taking the name of the Lord in vain. I think we take the name of the Lord in vain by our false praising. Sometimes when we come to God's house and sing and don't mean what we sing, we are taking the name of God in vain. "My Jesus, I love Thee, I know Thou art mine; For Thee all the follies of sin I resign; My gracious Redeemer, my Savior art thou; If ever I loved Thee, my Jesus 'tis now." Do you really mean that when you sing it? "Thou shalt not take the name of the Lord thy God in vain."

Here is the desecration of God's name. All of these Commandments, though they may be passed in a negative way, also have a positive emphasis. When the Bible says don't take the name of the Lord God in vain, you can take positively what Jesus said in the Model Prayer and use it here. "Hallowed be thy name." May your name be honored.

Think with me about

The *Declaration* of God's Name

Declare it as the Scripture teaches us to do. "Thou shalt call call his name Jesus; for he shall save his people from their sins" (Matt. 1:21). Acts 4:12 says, "Neither is there salvation in any other: for there is none other name under heaven given among men, whereby we must be saved." Romans 10:13 says, "For whosoever shall call upon the name of the Lord shall be saved." What a wonderful name—the name of Jesus. At the name of Jesus alcoholics can be made sober. Harlots can be made pure. At the name of Jesus infidels can be made believers. Addicts can be set free. What a wonderful name is the name of Jesus. Men, women, boys, and girls can call on that name and there is salvation in the name of Jesus.

Not only is there salvation in the name of Jesus, there is also strength in the name of Jesus. You and I have the privilege of serving in that name. Colossians 3:17 says, "And whatsoever ye do in word or deed, do all in the name of the Lord Jesus." We can sing in the name of Jesus and there's strength when we sing. We can preach in the name of Jesus and there is power when we preach. I don't preach in my name; I preach in the name of Jesus. When I preach there is power if I am preaching what the Word of God teaches and what the name of the Lord will confirm in the Scriptures. So, we serve in the name of Jesus. There is strength in that name. The Bible says if you give a cup of water in His name you'll not lose your reward (see Matt. 10:42). When the apostle Peter saw the crippled man at the gate of the temple, he said "In the name of Jesus Christ of Nazareth rise up and walk" (Acts 3:6). Jesus said, "In my name shall they cast out devils" (Mark 16:17).

We have the privilege of praying in His name. We can call on the name of Jesus in prayer. John 14:14 says, "If ye shall ask anything in my name, I will do it." In the sixteenth chapter Jesus said, "In that day ye shall ask me nothing. Verily, verily, I say unto you, Whatsoever ye shall ask the Father in my name, he will give it you. Hitherto have ye asked nothing in my name: ask and ye shall receive," (vv. 23–24). At that day you shall ask in My name. There's power when you pray in the name of Jesus. When you and I pray in Jesus' name we are saying that we are praying in the authority of Jesus. I am acting as His power of attorney. I am putting His name down to my prayer because I believe I am praying what Jesus would have done. You are praying with the approval of Jesus. Can you ask Jesus to approve the things you do? Can Jesus sign His precious name? There's strength in the name of Jesus.

There's safety in the name of Jesus. "The name of the Lord is a strong tower: the righteous runneth into it and is safe" (Prov. 18:10). There is safety in the name of the Lord. When temptation comes we can call on the name of Jesus. "When temptations round you gather, Breathe that holy name in pray'r." There is a name the devil can't stand and it's the name of Jesus. When the devil wants to tempt you to sin you just use that name of Jesus. Just mention His name and the devil will take flight.

We use the name of Jesus in times of sorrow. It is a healing balm. "How sweet the name of Jesus sounds In a believer's ear! It soothes his sorrows, heals his wounds, And drives away his fears." Many a heartbroken saint of God has taken solace and comfort and found safety and security in the name of Jesus.

General William Booth, the great founder of the Salvation Army, was very near death. His wife and children had some papers that needed his signature. The children went to him and said, "If you would just sign your name on these papers it would help us and facilitate some things that need to be done." He took the pen and signed the paper. Later when the family looked at it they saw he had signed the name of Jesus.

When you and I step into those chilly waters of death, legal papers aren't going to mean a whole lot to us either, but there will be a name that is above every name. It will be all-important to us. There is going to come a day when people won't blaspheme the name of Jesus. Philippians 2:10–11 says, "Wherefore God also hath highly exalted him, and given him a name which is above every name: That at the name of Jesus [won't be cussing, no profanity, no blaspheming] every knee should bow . . . And that every tongue should confess that Jesus Christ is Lord." That's the holy Name.

You need to call on that name of Jesus and be saved. "I know a soul that is steeped in sin, That no man's art can cure; But I know a Name, a Name, a Name that can make that life all pure."

One of these days we are going to get to the throne of Jesus and that will be the name that is above every name. "At the name of Jesus bowing, Falling prostrate at His feet, King of kings in heav'n we'll crown Him, When our journey is complete. Precious name, O how sweet! Hope of earth and joy of heav'n. Precious name, O how sweet! Hope of earth and joy of heav'n."

4
God's Day: Blessing or Burden

(vv. 8–11)

The Fourth Commandment brings to a conclusion those Commandments that have to do with our relationship to God. All four of these Commandments are tied together and tell us how we are to worship God. Commandment number one says that we are to worship Him only. Jesus said "Thou shalt worship the Lord thy God, and Him only shalt thou serve" (Matt. 4:10).

Commandment number two says that we are to worship Him correctly. We are not to make any graven images nor are we to bow down to any image of God.

Number three tells us that we are to worship God sincerely. The Scripture says, "Thou shalt not take the name of the Lord thy God in vain" (Ex. 20:7).

This Fourth Commandment teaches us that we are to worship the Lord regularly. "Remember the sabbath day, to keep it holy" (v. 8). This is the longest of all of the Commandments and it is probably the most misunderstood. There are some groups that make this particular teaching about the Sabbath Day the cornerstone of doctrine. There are some who gauge orthodoxy on whether or not one observes the Sabbath Day. I want to make it clear at the outset of this message that we are not worshiping on the Sabbath Day today. This is not the Sabbath Day. Yesterday, Saturday was the Sabbath Day. This is the first day—the Lord's Day. We are worshiping on Sunday, not on the Sabbath Day.

There is a reason why this is true and it will emerge as we study God's Word. As we look into this whole subject of keeping the Sabbath Day and what God has to say to us about it we will discover why we are worshiping on Sunday and not on Saturday— the Sabbath Day.

I want to first of all talk to you about

The *Explanation* of the Sabbath

There are generally two extremes when it comes to this whole matter of a day of worship. There are some who have historically and even to this day made the day of worship a day of gloom, burden, and misery. I read recently that back in the early years of our country in New England that a sea captain had been away for two years and was returning. His wife became so elated at his arrival that she ran from the house and hugged and kissed him and they promptly put her in jail because she was doing it on the Lord's Day.

So, there are some who interpret this Commandment to mean "Thou shalt be miserable on the Lord's Day." God never intended for His day to be a miserable day—to be a burden—to be a drag on His people.

The other extreme is to just make the Lord's Day any other day. It becomes just a day to go to the mall, or, just a day to work in the yard. A day to pack out the stadium. Many people today sacrifice this day on the altar of profit and pleasure. Someone said that our great grandfathers called it the holy Sabbath. Our grandfathers called it the Sabbath. Our fathers called it Sunday and we call it the weekend and it's getting weaker all the time. Somewhere between those two extremes I believe there is a place where God can take the day of worship and make it a day of tremendous blessing and benefit in your life.

The word *sabbath* is taken from the Hebrew word *shabbath* which means rest. It refers to a cessation from labor. It refers to a ceasing of work. Sabbath means rest. Some might ask, "Do you observe the Sabbath?" My response would be—which Sabbath are you talking about? When you study the Bible you will discover that here is not just one Sabbath but rather there are many. I'm going to go through a summary of at least seven Sabbaths that are taught in the Scriptures.

There is what I call the *initial* Sabbath. We find this in Genesis 2:1–3. That is the Sabbath where, after the Lord had created the heavens and the earth, the Bible says God rested on the seventh day. The Bible says He did two things that day. Number one, He blessed that day and number two, He sanctified it. He made it a special day. Of course, we know that when it says God rested that does not mean that God was weary. Isaiah 40:28 says that our God does not faint, neither is He weary. So, when God rested on the Sabbath Day, in commemoration of His work of creation, it was really a celebration. It was the climax, the completion of the fulfillment of His creative activity. That's the initial Sabbath taught in the Bible.

The second is what I call the *temporal* Sabbath. In Exodus 16:22–23; 20:8 in the Ten Commandments and again in 31:17 we are told about this temporal Sabbath. This day is the day that God gave.

In Exodus 31:17 we are specifically taught that the Sabbath Day was a sign between the Lord and the children of Israel. You will find in the New Testament all of the other Ten Commandments are reiterated in some form or another. But we do not find the Sabbath Day reiterated there because the Sabbath Day was given specifically to Israel to commemorate the creative activity of God.

Number three, there was the *festival* Sabbath. In Leviticus 23:23–36 we are told there was to be a festival Sabbath at the beginning of the Feast of the Trumpets and also at the Feast of the Tabernacles. For instance, the Feast of the Trumpets was in the seventh month on the first day of the month. The Feast of the Tabernacles was on the fifteen day of the month. It was a festival Sabbath. It was to be observed yearly. Notice something in that connection. If it was to be observed on the first day and fifteenth day of the month yearly, that means not every year did that festival Sabbath occur on Saturday. That brings us to a very important point. Every Saturday is a Sabbath, but not every Sabbath is a Saturday. There is the festival Sabbath.

Number four, there is an agricultural Sabbath taught in the Old Testament. In Leviticus 25:1–8 God commanded the children of Israel that they were to work the land for six years and the seventh year was to be a Sabbath year. The land was not to be cultivated in that Sabbath year. One year out of seven the land was not to be cultivated. The Scripture tells us that Israel failed to do what God said to do. Israel did not keep that agricultural Sabbath. They were in the land for 490 years. That means that they missed that seventh year seventy times. When you come to Leviticus 26:32,35 God said that when He sent His children of Israel into captivity that they would be there one year for every year they failed to observe an agricultural Sabbath. That's why they were in captivity for seventy years. God meant what He said to his children when He told them to keep an agricultural Sabbath.

The fifth is what I call the spiritual Sabbath. That's found in Hebrews 3 and 4. I'll come back to that later.

The sixth sabbath taught in the Old Testament is the millennial Sabbath. In Isaiah 66:22–23 we are told that during the millennium the children of Israel will once again restore the Sabbath.

The seventh Sabbath is the eternal Sabbath. Hebrews 4:9 says: "There remaineth therefore a rest to the people of God." Revelation 14:13 says, "Blessed are the dead which die in the Lord from henceforth: Yea, saith the Spirit, that they may rest from their labors." God predicts that one day you and I will be through with all of the burdens and all of the battles, all of the trials and all of the tribulations, and we will experience an eternal Sabbath in the presence of the Lord.

So, if somebody asks if I observe the Sabbath, my answer is— Which Sabbath are you talking about? That's the explanation of the Sabbath in the Scriptures.

Let's move on to

The *Transformation* of the Sabbath

When you get to the New Testament you become aware that a transformation has occurred. As you move out of the New Testament you will discover that believers in the New Testament economy are worshiping on the Lord's Day, not on the Sabbath Day. A transformation has occurred. When the Lord Jesus came the Bible says that He was born of a woman and made under the law. Jesus Christ perfectly fulfilled the law. Jesus obeyed the law in every detail. That's why we are told in the New Testament, for instance, that on the Sabbath Day as His custom was, Jesus went up to the synagogue. (See Luke 4:16.) Jesus Christ was faithful to observe the Sabbath. Yet, when you study the Gospels you will find that there was a running battle between the Pharisees and the Lord Jesus about this whole question of Sabbath observance. I had never really realized it until I started researching the Scriptures on just how much the Pharisees pushed Jesus on this whole point of Sabbath observing.

Jesus kept the Sabbath. What was the problem? If Jesus kept the Sabbath why did the Pharisees get all out of joint with Jesus? The Pharisees had taken the Sabbath and so loaded it down with man-made additions that it had become a tremendous burden. There are thirty-nine Hebrew words in the Fourth Commandment—*Remember the sabbath day, holy.* They took those thirty-nine words, multiplied them by thirty-nine, and came up with 1,521 things you couldn't do on the Sabbath Day. They made life miserable.

For instance, you couldn't rescue a drowning man on the Sabbath Day. You couldn't even fight a flea on the Sabbath Day. If a flea bit you they said you couldn't fight back because that would be fighting on the Sabbath Day and that was against the rules. You couldn't rescue an animal on the Sabbath Day. That would be totally unholy. You couldn't travel or cook a meal on the Sabbath Day. It just goes on and on.

When Jesus came you will discover in the New Testament that He laid aside all man-made rules. He disregarded all of their human ordinances and laws and Jesus made of the Sabbath Day what the Father had intended for it to be.

Let me just summarize some of the things Jesus taught about the Sabbath Day. Jesus said in Mark 2:27 "the sabbath was made for man, and not man for the sabbath." The Pharisees had made the means the end. They became more occupied with the means to the end than the end itself. What God intended to be a blessing and a benefit to mankind they had turned into a tremendous burden.

Another thing Jesus taught was that it was all right to do good on the Sabbath Day. He healed people on the Sabbath Day. One poor old woman had been bound over by an unclean spirit for eighteen years and the Lord Jesus Christ healed her and she straightened up on that day. The Pharisees accused Him and Jesus said, "Why, you loosen oxen on the Sabbath Day, can't I loose this woman who has been bound by Satan for eighteen years on the Sabbath Day?" (See Luke 13:11–16.) His disciples got hungry on the Sabbath Day, while walking through a field. They plucked some grains of corn and rubbed them together. The Pharisees got their noses all out of joint about it but the Lord Jesus Christ rebuked them. It was perfectly all right for the men to eat on the Sabbath Day. (See Mark 2:23–26.) You go right on through and you will discover that

Jesus says, "The Son of man is Lord also of the sabbath" (v.28). There is a transformation that occurs.

We worship on the Lord's Day. Why is it that you and I gather here on Sunday? When you begin to study this matter you will discover several things. Let me just show you the things that occur on the Lord's Day—the first day of the week. Jesus was resurrected on the first day (Mark 16:2,9). The disciples gathered together in the upper room on the first day (v. 11). They met on the Lord's Day that night (John 20:19–20). The Great Commission was given on the Lord's Day—the first day (Matt. 28:19–20). The Day of Pentecost occurred on the first day (Acts 2:1). The Holy Spirit was sent down on the first day (vv. 1–4). The apostle Paul preached the Word to believers on the first day (20:7). A collection was to be taken weekly in the house of God among the people of God on the first day (1 Cor. 16:2). John received from the Lord His revelation, completing the canon of Scripture, on the first day which he calls in Revelation 1:10 "the Lord's Day." So a transformation has occurred. A beautiful transformation it is indeed.

I want to show you three things that were transformed in the New Testament about this day of worship. Turn to Colossians 2. I want us to see that there is a transformation from shadow to substance. "Blotting out the handwriting of ordinances that was against us, which was contrary to us, and took it out of the way, nailing it to his cross" (v. 14). "Let no man therefore judge you in meat, or in drink, or in respect of an holy day, or of the new moon, or of the sabbath days: Which are a shadow of things to come; but the body [the reality, the fulfillment, the substance] is of Christ" (v. 16). He is simply saying that all of this was in the shadow. All the Old Testament was just a shadow announcing the arrival of future events. When the reality comes, you don't have to cling to the shadow anymore.

It's as if your wife has been gone for a few days and she gets off the plane and you go to meet her. As she stands there, you are on your way to meet her. You see both her and her shadow. Do you run over to the shadow and start hugging the shadow? There stands your wife in the flesh and you are all caught up with a shadow instead of the reality.

You and I are living now in the New Testament, in the reality of the gospel of the Lord Jesus Christ. When God created the world the Bible says He finished His work. When He finished His work, He rested—a rest of creation. When the Lord Jesus died on Calvary's cross John 19:3 says He said, "It is finished." That means He completed His redemption work. The reality now is in the finished work of Jesus Christ on Calvary's cross. Those who would insist that you worship on Saturday and not on Sunday are on the wrong side of Calvary. We have the reality now in the Lord Jesus Christ. That which the Old Testament pointed to is now ours in the Lord Jesus Christ. There's a transformation from shadow to substance.

There is also a transformation from Saturday to Sunday. Turn to Romans 14. The apostle Paul is dealing here with matters about which Christians may differ. "One man esteemeth one day above another [some people get hung up with a day]: another esteemeth every day alike. Let every man be fully persuaded in his own mind. He that regardeth the day, regardeth it unto the Lord; and he that regardeth not the day, to the Lord he doth not regard it" (vv. 5–6). Paul is simply saying that the day is not the point. You don't even really know what today is. But, the calendar has has changed so many times through the centuries we really don't know what day it is today. It could be Tuesday for all we know. It could be Friday. You might be getting ready to get off from work on a Friday. You don't know what day it is. It really doesn't matter what day it is. You and I are meeting on Sunday because we believe we celebrate the resurrection of Jesus today. That seems to be the New Testament pattern. But if you want to worship on Saturday, that's fine, too. "Let every man be fully persuaded in his own mind." The point is not the particular day. The point is that you set aside a day when you do what God commands you to do on a very special day. So, there's a transformation from shadow to substance. There's a transformation from Saturday to Sunday.

There's a transformation from Sabbath to the Savior. Hebrews 3 and 4 are the primary statements in the New Testament which indicate to us the transformation that has occurred from the Sabbath to the Lord's Day—the first day of the week. You will discover in Hebrews 4:9–11 there is a threefold rest—a threefold Sabbath, if you please, a spiritual Sabbath that is taught in these verses. For instance, verse 10, "For he that is entered into his rest, he also has ceased from his own works, as God did from his." Look at the third verse of that chapter—"For we which have believed [those of us who have received Jesus and repented of sin and by faith invited Him into our heart] do enter into rest." That's what he's talking about in verse 10. He that has entered into his rest has ceased from his own works. In the Old Testament they worked and then they rested. In salvation we rest in the finished work of Jesus and then we work. You don't work in order to be saved. You work because you are saved. "I dare not work my soul to save, that work my Lord has done. But I will work like any slave for love of God's dear son." There is the past rest we have because we are trusting in the finished work of Jesus Christ.

In verse 9 is the prospective rest. "There remaineth therefore a rest to the people of God." I've referred to this already. One of these days there is going to be a perfect rest. Every day will be Sunday by and by. Every day we will be in the presence of Jesus and we'll worship Him perfectly, enjoy Him fully, will comprehend Him, and understand Him in ever unfolding revelations of His love and grace. There's that prospective rest.

Look at the present rest—verse 11. "Let us labor therefore to enter into that rest, lest any man fall after the same example of unbelief." He says we have entered into rest and now he says let us labor to enter into that rest. You will understand it when you get what Jesus said in Matthew 11:28—"Come unto me, all ye that labor and are heavy laden, and I will give you rest." That's the rest of salvation. We need not only to rest in Jesus Christ for our salvation. We need to rest in Jesus Christ for our daily sanctification and service. That's why Jesus said in the next verse: "Take my yoke upon you, and learn of me; for I am meek and lowly in heart; and ye shall find rest unto your souls" (v. 29). Day by day, as we serve the Lord Jesus, we can learn to rest in Him. The work does not depend upon us; it depends upon Him. When we gather on the Lord's Day we celebrate resurrection, but we also recognize the fact that all of our labors are in vain unless we labor in the Lord.

The *Application of the Sabbath Day*

If the Sabbath is in the Old Testament, what application does Sabbath teaching have for us today? I believe the application is at least threefold for you and me as born-again, New Testament believers.

It has a personal application. In Exodus 20:8 God says to keep the Sabbath Day holy, make it a special day. Then He says in verses 9–10, "Six days shalt thou labor, and do all thy work: But the seventh day is the sabbath of thy Lord thy God: in it thou shalt not do any work,..." Notice the shift from labor to leisure. "Six days shalt thou labor." God has a message to us about the importance of labor. Don't ever get the idea that work was something that came as a result of sin in the garden of Eden. It did not. Genesis 2:15 says that God put Adam in the garden "to dress it and keep it" (that is, to cultivate it). Work was a gift of God to mankind.

Work is the way God has devised for people to uncover all of the treasures God has provided for them in this world. The sweat-of-your-brow kind of work—work with difficulty—occurred after sin in Genesis 3. There God said that man would now work by the sweat of his brow. He'll get weary in his work. There's nothing wrong with work, though. God says we are to work. By the way, I believe we ought to help those who can't help themselves. The Bible says the strong ought to support the weak. We ought to make provision for and care for those who are not able to provide for themselves. But it is a sin to help people who are unwilling to work when they are able.

Where did you get that, Preacher? I got it out of the Bible in 2 Thessalonians 3:10. "If any would not work, neither should he eat." I know that will upset some of the bleeding-heart liberals in the world, but that's what the Book says. That's not Vines, that's Bible. You let some of the loafers who aren't willing to work get hungry enough and they will work. In America, when half of the population gets the idea that they can eat and not work and the other half of the population gets the idea that though they work they do not enjoy the fruits of their labors, you are in trouble in this country. And that's exactly where we are now. One of the greatest cures in the world for poverty is good, old-fashioned hard work. It's honorable.

Jesus worked as a carpenter. He wasn't a namby-pamby sissy. If you had seen the hands of the Lord Jesus Christ you would have seen calluses. Jesus was a carpenter. He picked up big pieces of wood and worked in that carpenter shop with His own hands. Jesus honored work. So, this Commandment has something to do with the importance of labor.

Then notice it also has something to do with the importance of leisure. God says you are to work six days but then the seventh day you are to take off. Do you ever feel guilty when you aren't working? Has anyone ever accused you of being a workaholic? Do you ever bring your briefcase home and work a little on Sunday to catch up? The Lord says we are to take a day of leisure. There is a rhythm to life. We see it in the natural world. There is a day and there is a night. There is cold and hot weather. There is a sense of balance in life and God says, "I have given you a special day—take a day off." You say, "I'm too busy, I can't take a day off." God created the heavens and earth and He took a day off. There's nothing wrong with taking a day off. Have a day to rest.

How many of you take a nap on Sunday? That's good for you, rests your body. On Sunday you ought to refresh your body. It has been proven scientifically that people are a lot better off physically if they take a day to rest. You really do not, just in a night's sleep, recoup enough oxygen. You really need a day when you relax your body to recoup all of the oxygen you have expended in a six-day workweek.

When I was living in Georgia, ten miles from my hometown was Bremen. That's where a lot of clothing is made. Once a pants factory was working for seven days. They finally decided to take off a day and rest those machines. They found out the machines in the factory lasted longer when they rested them one day. That's a fact. Your body will last longer if you will take off a day to rest.

I heard about a little town in Scotland where they decided to pipe some water from a magnificent lake on the top of a mountain just above the town. They installed the pipes to bring the water down to the little village, but the pipes burst because of the tremendous pressure of the flow of the water. So, along the way, down the mountain, they set reservoirs. Instead of just coming down in one constant stream the water came from reservoir to reservoir to reservoir. They found that when the water had a resting place along the way it did a lot better. You will do a whole lot better if you will take some time to refresh your body. Take a little time on the Lord's Day to restore your soul. David said in Psalm 23:3, "He restoreth my soul."

I heard about some natives that were leading a group through the jungles of Africa. They had been going for six days and on the seventh day the natives refused to walk. They said, "We have to have a day to let our souls catch up with our bodies." You need a day to restore your soul. Something else, you need a day to renew your spirit. It has personal applications. It also has social applications.

Jesus said you can do good on this day. He healed sick people. He helped people on the Sabbath Day. It was evidently a great time of fellowship. Jesus went into the homes and ate with people on the Sabbath Day, that day of rest. There are some of you who are in occupations of service. Some of you are doctors who have to work on Sunday. I work on Sunday. This is not a day of rest for me. My day begins early Sunday morning. To be perfectly frank, when Sunday is over I feel like I've been run over by a big truck. Sunday is not a day of rest for me. Some folks work on Sunday because of necessity.

But there may be opportunities for some of you on Sunday to visit a sick person or maybe help someone in need. When I was a teenage boy and God had called me to preach, I went to the prison on Sunday afternoon. Every Sunday afternoon I preached in the prison.

I don't do anything on Sunday afternoon now. If three-thousand-plus of you are going to show up Sunday night I want to be fresh and ready. When you get my age you aren't as fresh as you were when you were sixteen. So, I don't preach in the prison on Sunday afternoon. But it has social applications—do good, help people, be a blessing on the Lord's Day.

It also has devotional applications. There needs to be one day of the week where we gather in the Lord's house. I want to compliment you for being in God's house on a Sunday night. Sunday night is special to me. I was saved on a Sunday night. I was sitting on a second row when the preacher preached. God's Spirit dealt with my heart and I was saved. Great time to get saved—Sunday night. Give God all of His day, be in His house for Sunday School, be in His house for morning worship, be in His house for discipleship training, be in His house for the Sunday night service. We need one day a week to get away from the fog of this old world to observe the bright lights of the glory world. We need one day to get away from the voice of business and hear the voice of God. We need one day to get away from the noise, clamor, and clutter of the business world and hear the sweet strains of songs of praise to our Lord God, our wonderful, wonderful Savior.

So, we take a day to worship the Lord. We take a day to rest the body. We take a day to try to be a blessing to someone else. You say, ''Preacher I have a list of things I want to ask you about the Lord's day. Is it all right to do these things on the Lord's Day? It is all right to go to a ball game on the Lord's Day? Is it all right to watch a ball game on TV on the Lord's Day? Is it right to do this and that?'' The only problem with that is that you have brought your list to the wrong person. The Scripture does not say Jerry Vines is the Lord of the Sabbath. Mark 2:28 says, ''The Son of man is the Lord also of the sabbath.'' So, bring your list to the Lord of the Sabbath and ask Him what he wants you to do on that day. Whatever you do be sure that you make the day a blessing and not a burden. Be sure you make it a day of rest. Have you ever seen people coming in from the beaches on a Sunday night—how tired they are? Ever seen people come in to work on a Monday morning and just dragging in? Be sure you take some time to rest. Be sure you take some time on the Lord's Day to be a blessing to someone else.

5
Honor Your Parents
(v. 12)

A newspaper editor decided he would print one of the Ten Commandments every day for ten successive days in his newspaper. At the completion of his listing of the Ten Commandments a reader wrote in and said, "Cancel my subscription. Your paper is getting too personal." We are going to get very, very personal now in the sermons to follow because these Commandments treat our relationships with one another. You will remember that the Ten Commandments were given by God to Moses on tablets of stone. The two tablets of stone remind us that these Commandments have to do with the two vital relationships of life. The first four commandments deal with man's relationship to God. The next six Commandments are about man's relationship to his fellowman.

These two belong together. You can't be right with your fellowman if you are not right with God. If you are right with God, then you are in a position to be right with your fellowman. The Lord Jesus summarized all the Ten Commandments this way when He said, (1) "Thou shalt love the Lord thy God" and (2) ". . . love thy neighbor as thyself" (Matt. 2:37,39). These two great sections of the Ten Commandments hang together. They belong to one another— our relationship to God and our relationship with one another.

They also tie together religion and morality. In my reading and watching and listening to the media, I am finding that many people recognize the fact that we need to return to teaching some kind of values and morals in our schools. I certainly applaud that. By the way, I'm grateful for those in our school system who are believers, those who are Christian teachers. I applaud them for their efforts. Really, we are assigning our schools an impossible task. You cannot teach morality apart from religion.

So, we kicked Bible reading out of the schools. Then, when we threw prayer out of the schools, we made it almost impossible to teach morals. You cannot teach right from wrong apart from the standards that are revealed in the Word of God. So these tie together—religion, our relationship to God; morals—our relationship to one another.

Another truth you will notice is: in these Ten Commandments God has given—in crystal-clear, simple, easy-to-understand language—basic morality. Today there is a great deal of moral ambiguity—uncertainty in contemporary morals. *Maybe* it's right; *maybe* it's wrong. *Maybe* you can; *maybe* you can't. When you read the Ten Commandments you will find that God gives moral absolutes. With a few words, in these Commandments God establishes acceptable human behavior—not only for that day, not only for our day, but for all time and eternity.

We are going to look now at these Commandments that deal with our relationships toward one another. It is interesting and instructive to recognize that the first of these having to do with our relationships to others is the Commandment which says "Honor thy father and thy mother." The first *others* you run into are your mom and your dad. So, you need to learn to get along with your mother and father. If you can't learn to get along with your family, then you are going to have problems getting along with anybody else in society. The family is the basic structure of human civilization. It all begins right here. So, God in His infinite wisdom begins by saying "Honor thy father and thy mother." I have a very simple outline which will be easy for you to follow. There are three basic facts I want us to study. Number one, the parents, number two, the precept, and number three, the promise.

The *Parents*
"Honor thy father and thy mother."

Think for a moment about the role of being a parent. Being a parent is, first of all:

A Biological Matter

Mothers and fathers have made it possible for us to have existence. Kids, you didn't have a thing in the world to do with choosing your parents—no choice in the matter. You didn't have a vote. You didn't go to a store, see moms and dads on display, and choose one. Your parents may have more hang-ups than the phone company. On the other side of that coin, kids, your parents didn't choose you, either. For all you know, your mom and dad may go to PTA meetings under an assumed name! You got them, and they got you. I want to encourage you about this matter of your parents.

Once upon a time you were one out of 50 million sperm cells, all lined up in a long canal in a race to locate an egg cell. Out of all those 50 million cells—congratulations—you won the race. You came into existence. Don't think for a moment that that was an accident. Psalm 139:14–16 says:

> I will praise thee; for I am fearfully and wonderfully made: marvelous are thy works; and that my soul knoweth right well. My substance was not hid from thee, when I was made in secret, and curiously wrought in the lowest parts of the earth. Thine eyes did see my substance, yet being unperfect; and in thy book all my members were written.

When you were conceived God was there, and God allowed you to be born to the mother and the father you have.

So birth and parenthood are a biological matter. This means, as a parent, you have the responsibility for the physical care of your children. Biologically you gave them life. Now you have responsibility to guard them, to care for them, and to meet their needs biologically and physically. It's wonderful when you think about parents who are willing to provide for their children.

I heard about a boy at school who was talking to a friend. He said, "I'm really worried."

His friend asked, "What are you worried about?"

He said, "My dad just works so hard, works overtime to provide for the needs of our home. Mom washes the clothes, prepares the meals, and keeps the house clean."

His friend said, "What in the world are you worried about?"

The boy replied, "I'm afraid they might escape." Think about how wonderful it is that you have parents who are willing to do this for you, Kids.

I heard about a boy who presented his mother a bill. It said:

"Washing the car—$5.00. Taking out the garbage—$5.00. Total bill you owe me—$10.00." The next meal the mother had put a bill on his plate, also. It said: "Washing your clothes—$5.00. Preparing your meal—$5.00. Taking care of you when sick—$5.00. Getting you to school on time—$5.00. Total bill—I love you."

Isn't it marvelous that you have someone in this world who loves you and is interested in you? God has given to every child a superb gift—parents who grant them the gift of life. Parents are able to give their children a quality of life that no one else can really offer them. It includes the gift of experience. One of the reasons children have parents is because parents have experience. They are supposed to know some things you don't.

A father instructed his daughter, "Listen, you be in from your date by 11:00 tonight."

She argued, "Dad, I'm not a child, you know."

He came back, "I know, that's why I said be in by 11:00 tonight!"

Your parents have been along the road you are traveling. It's as if they are driving to Los Angeles with you not far behind them. When they reach Phoenix they make a phone call to you. They advise, "You need to watch out for this road—it's under repair. Better take a detour here. You ought to try this restaurant along the way. It's a good place to eat. Don't stay in this motel—it's a dump." The fact that they have already been down the road means that they can give you helpful advice and counsel along the way. That's what every parent ought to do. You ought to give to your children the benefit of your experience along the way.

An Emotional Matter

So, being a parent is a biological matter. It is also *an emotional matter*. It's not enough simply to bring children into this world. It is not because you can produce a baby that qualifies you to be a parent. Being able to produce a baby biologically does not mean you are a successful parent or that you are qualified to be one. There is also an emotional responsibility to be a parent.

It's as if someone placed a diamond in your hand. You are asked to engrave one sentence on that diamond. Be very careful what you write—it will be on that diamond the rest of its existence. When God gives you a child, He has placed a precious diamond in your hand. On that diamond you will write a sentence. Be careful, moms and dads, what you write. It will go with them the rest of their lives.

What our boys and girls become emotionally, to a great extent, will be what you and I as parents have engraved upon their psyches. We have a responsibility to love our children, and give them emotional support. We are to lead our children. Then, when the day comes, we are to let loose of our children with our hopes, ambitions, and prayers.

Being a parent is *a biological matter*—"Honor thy father and thy mother." Being a parent is *an emotional matter*. Honor your father and your mother. Being a parent is *a spiritual matter,* also. It's not enough merely to meet physical needs. It's not sufficient to meet emotional needs only—but you, also, as a parent have responsibility to meet their *spiritual* needs.

A Spiritual Matter

The first concept a child has of God is picked up from their parents. Sometimes when I read the Model Prayer and see that our Lord taught us to begin prayer by saying "Our Father," I shudder when I read that in our twentieth century the first concept children have of God is from their earthly parents. Parents are like a skylight or a prism through which a child sees his first view of God. What an awesome responsibility before God it is to be a parent! The Bible teaches parents are to be responsible for the religious training of their children. Thank God for Sunday School and for faithful Sunday School teachers, but the basic responsibility for spiritual training of your boys and girls is yours.

I think every parent ought to have a family altar. You had better do it when the kids are little. When they have "wheels" of their own, they will be gone. It will be really hard to do it then. Start off teaching the Scriptures when they are little. Have a daily Bible reading time with your boys and girls. When you read the Letters of Paul, have you noticed Paul wrote words of greeting to "the church that is in their house" (Rom. 16:5; also see Col. 4:15). Have you ever thought about that statement? I wonder if Paul were writing today would he say "to the cafeteria in thy house" or "to the amusement center in thy house" or "to the closet in thy house"? There ought to be a church in your house where mom and dad have the Word of God, gather the family together, read and study that Word, and pray together.

The University of Chicago did a survey of its graduate students asking them where they received their clearest teachings or impressions concerning religion and morality. The majority of those students answered that they picked up their concepts of religion and morality from the mealtime conversations of their families. Think about it. Parents, your number-one responsibility is to lead those boys and girls to accept Jesus Christ as their personal Savior. I care not if you are the president of the largest corporation in this city tonight—if you don't lead your children to Jesus Christ, you are a failure! No person is a failure who wins his/her family to Jesus Christ.

Noah was "a preacher of righteousness." He preached for 120 years, and the people mocked him and ridiculed him. "Crazy Noah—building a boat; never has rained." Yet, one day when the rains of judgment began to fall, the Bible records that Noah and his wife, his sons and their wives all entered the ark of safety. No person is a failure who can lead his family into the ark of safety. This Commandment declares, "Honor thy father and thy mother."

The *Precept*— "Honor"

Here is the Commandment: "Honor thy father and thy mother." In the New Testament you find this repeated. In Ephesians 6:1–3 it occurs again. "Children, obey your parents in the Lord: for this is right. Honor thy father and mother which is the first commandment with promise; That it may be well with thee, and thou mayest live long on the earth." Paul emphasizes that it is right for children to obey and honor their parents. Colossians 3:20 says, "Children, obey your parents in all things: for this is well pleasing unto the Lord." Notice it is right—it is well pleasing to the Lord—to honor one's parents.

The word *honor* means "to give weight to," to hold in high esteem. As Paul lays it out in Ephesians 6, there is a twofold application of the command to honor one's mother and father.

There is, first of all, the matter of obedience, and then, the matter of honor. "Obey your parents." This teaches that the children are to respond to their parents. "Obey your parents in the Lord." The word *obey* literally means "to hear under." It carries the concept of authority. The children in the family are to answer to the authority of their parents. God has established authority in every realm of life. There is authority in government, authority in church, authority in the family.

Obey your parents. Listen to your parents. It is the responsibility of parents to teach the child obedience because, in so doing, they teach the child to obey authority wherever he finds it. If you as a parent fail to teach your children to obey you, that simply means: everywhere they go they will have problems. If you don't teach them to obey you in your home, when they go to school they will have problems obeying the teacher. When they go out into society they will have problems obeying the officials and the established authority of government. When they go to work, and a supervisor tells them what to do, they are going to have problems responding to that authority. Why? They have never learned authority.

One of the saddest fallouts of the entire rock-music scene— starting back in the late 1950s and early 1960s—is that the underlying theme of rebellion against parents caught hold of a generation of young people, and it became difficult for the baby-boomer generation to accept the concept of authority. It has caused all kinds of problems. So, you have a responsibility to teach your boys and girls to obey—teaching them to respond to you, to listen to you, and to obey you, "in the Lord."

You say, "Do I obey my parents under every circumstance?" The Word says obey them in the Lord. If your parents tell you to kill somebody, obviously you don't obey. If your parents tell you to steal something, certainly you don't obey. You obey *in the Lord*. A parent is called on to be the kind that makes it easy for the children to obey him/her. A parent must be the type of parent the child will love and respect enough to obey.

Colossians 3:21—"Fathers, provoke not your children to anger, lest they be discouraged." The word *discouraged* means "to lose heart," to give up. Is it impossible for your children to please you? If they make C's, they ought to have made B's. If they make B's, they ought to have made A's. If they make A's, they ought to have made *all* A's. Sometimes if parents are unpleaseable, impossible, the Scripture indicates that children lose heart. They give up. "What's the use?" they ask. Parents need to balance criticism with praise. There ought to be more strokes than pokes, more bragging than nagging. Your children learn what you teach them at home. If you teach them criticism, they learn to condemn. If you teach them hostility, they learn to fight. If you teach them shame, they learn to feel guilt. If you teach them tolerance, they learn patience. If you teach them patience, they learn to be understanding. If you teach them praise, they learn to be appreciative. If you teach them security they learn to trust. You have a great deal to do with whether or not your children obey you. Parents are to respond. That simply puts the primary responsibility on the parent.

Respect for Parents

The Commandment says to honor your father and your mother. It does not say "honor your father and your mother until you are eighteen." The concept of honor goes on beyond the so-called age of adolescence. One of these days most of you kids are going to be married. When you do, you will then establish your home, a new center of authority. You will no longer be under the authority of your parents, but the command to honor your parents continues on beyond the time you are no longer under their authority. "Honor thy father and thy mother."

What if my parents are not honorable? What if one's parents are not worthy of being honored? Sometimes a person goes to court, stands in front of a bench, and addresses the judge "Your Honor." That doesn't say a thing about the kind of individual that judge is. People acknowledge the authority of his position as judge. The Bible commands you to honor your parents, if nothing else, for the fact that they are your parents.

By the way, Kids, there are no perfect parents. Only perfect children have a right to demand perfect parents! Children normally pass through four stages in their relationship to their parents. The first stage is when they *idolize* their parents. "Daddy can do anything. He can get me the moon if I need it." When they reach the point where they realize their mom and dad are not perfect, then they *demonize* their parents. Mom and dad are the source of all of the miseries and all of the troubles of the world. Then the kids become a little bit smarter and move into the stage where they *utilize* their parents. "Dad, how about the keys to the car?" "Mom, how about you doing dishes?" They use their parents.

If you grow to the maturity God desires for you, you will arrive at the fourth stage where you will *humanize* your parents. You will realize they are neither God nor the devil—not things to be used, but humans, and have their strong and weak points just like you.

Think about it, for all their faults, they probably made some real sacrifices for you. Who else would put up with you as they did? Have you ever thought about what your parents may have sacrificed for you? Because they have you, there are trips they may have passed up. There is money they could have spent on themselves. Instead, they have spent it on you—for clothes, for school, for your expenses, maybe even wheels. They are also spending that money on doctor bills and other care for you.

Honor your father and your mother. There may be some fifty-year-old children who need to forgive parents. You need to acknowledge they had their faults and weren't perfect, and quit holding animosity in your heart against them. "You don't know what they did to me." It's not important what they did to you; what is important is how you responded to what your parents did. Some of you kids may be ashamed of your parents right now. You don't even want your friends around because you are embarrassed by your parents. Your friends may admire and respect you because they know you have a tough time, but if you are living for Jesus in a difficult situation, they will admire you for being the kind of young person you are in tough circumstances.

Throw away your magnifying glass. Quit expecting perfection out of your parents. Honor your father and your mother. That is the Commandment that continues all the days of your life. When you grow older, the roles have a tendency to reverse themselves. There comes a point where the children almost assume the role of the parent, and the parent steps into the role of the child. The Bible teaches that you have responsibility to care for your parents. Look at 1 Timothy 5:4. "But if any widow have children or nephews, let them learn first to show piety at home." Paul was saying if you claim to have religion and don't have it at home, you are a sham. You can't play "goody two-shoes" around the church, and then act like the devil at home. The Bible says to "show piety at home." Be a Christian at home.

My dear, sweet mother was a very quiet woman. When God called me to preach as a sixteen-year-old boy, I was the first young person ever called to preach from our church. I was "the preacher boy." I was considered important. I had a halo around my head at church. To be perfectly honest with you I sometimes discarded that halo at home. One day I was not being what I should be around the house, and my sweet, quiet little mother said to me, "If you're going to be the preacher around the church, why don't you start being the preacher around the house?" She was exactly right. If you haven't got it at home, Kids, you haven't got it at church. "Learn first to show piety at home, and to requite [pay back] their parents: for that is good and acceptable before God."

There may come a time when you will even have to render financial assistance to your parents, a day when you will have to minister to the needs of your parents. I had a meal with a man and his mother recently. This lady told me about having cared for and ministered to her mother who had died not long before. In all those years she had faithfully cared for her mother. God bless you folks who are caring for and helping your parents. You will be so glad you did it.

Mark's Gospel records that Jesus once called the Pharisees a bunch of hypocrites. He stated when you have an opportunity to do something for your parents you call that money "Corban," which means "devoted to God" (see 7:6–13). He was saying you use the money you gave to church as an excuse for not taking care of your parents. Honor your mother and your father.

Some of you ought to phone and/or write your parents. You ought to thank them. We are to obey them in our younger years. We are to support them in their older years. We are to honor them in all their years.

The first point was the *parents*. The second point was the *precept*. The third point is:

The *Promise*

As Paul noted in Ephesians 6:2 this Fifth Commandment is the first commandment with a promise attached to it. Go back to Exodus 20:12 which says "Honor thy father and thy mother: that thy days may be long upon the land which the Lord thy God giveth thee." There is a promise attached. Let me give you the primary meaning of that promise. It was to the children of Israel concerning the land of Canaan—a national promise to the Hebrews that, if they would be obedient and would honor their parents, God would bless them with long life in the Promised Land. That is certainly true from a national perspective. Show me a nation where there is disobedience to parents, and I will show you a nation whose foundations are crumbling. No nation is going to last very long that is characterized by disobedience to parents.

In the Book of Romans Paul laid out the characteristics of the depraved human heart. Right in the midst of murder, and all of those heinous sins he lists in verse 30 of Chapter 1, is disobedience to parents. In Timothy 3:2, where he catalogs the characteristics of the depravity and decadence of the last days, he also says, "disobedience to parents." America has yet to pick up the change we are due on a generation that has been brought up in disobedience to parents. This has been a serious sin of rebellion. It was so severe that when there was an incorrigible child, disobedient to parents, who could not be changed, the Old Testament Scripture says they took the child out and stoned him to death. That's how serious is the sin of disobedience to parents.

Remember Eli in the Old Testament and his wayward sons. Their story is given in I Samuel 2. "The sons of Eli were sons of Belial; they knew not the Lord" (v. 12). God said about the sons of Eli: "There shall not be an old man in thine house" (v. 31). God was teaching, if you don't honor your parents, if you are not obedient to your parents, you are not going to live long in the land which the Lord thy God giveth thee. That is the primary application.

Then there is the secondary application. Honor your parents that your life may be long upon the earth. That young person who learns to be obedient to parents has established a pattern in life that will tend to longevity of life. Young people who establish patterns of rebellion, disobedience, and disrespect to their parents have established habits that tend to a short, trouble-filled life.

You ask, "What about a child who is a sweet Christian child? They love their parents, they obey their parents, they live for Jesus. They are everything in this world you could expect a Christian young person to be in relationship to their parents, and they are suddenly snuffed out. What about this promise?"

Let me show you what God showed me. I had never seen it before. The greatest example of the fulfillment of this Fifth Commandment is found in the life of Jesus Christ, our Lord. When He was a child the Bible says He went down with Mary and Joseph to

Nazareth and He "was subject unto them" (Luke 2:51). That's the only child who ever knew more than His parents, and yet He was subject to them. Yet, when Jesus became a man, He honored His mother. On the cross He looked at John the beloved disciple and said to His mother, "Woman, behold thy son" (John 19:26). He said to John, "Behold they mother" (v. 27). John took Mary, the mother of the Lord Jesus Christ, to his home and took care of her. Jesus Christ honored His mother. Yet, the One who most perfectly fulfilled this Commandment did not live a long life. What does that have to do with the promise? If you had a sweet, Christian young person in your home who through some tragedy was snuffed out, it simply would mean this: Jesus did not live a long time because the Father had a work for Him to do in His death that could not be done otherwise. Somehow in the grace and providence of God that precious child of yours who went on to heaven had a work that could not be done in any other way except in death.

I heard evangelist Jess Hendley tell this. I think it helps people who have lost dear loved ones in death. Hendley said there was a gardener who was tending roses for his master. There was one rose in particular that was special to the master, and the master had assigned the gardener to care for that beautiful white rose. How he cared for it—fertilized it, pruned it, trimmed it, and watered it. That white rose was blossoming.

One day the gardener walked through the garden, and the white rose was gone. He looked everywhere for it. He was frantic. He was going to give the bad news that the master's prize white rose was gone. He walked into the master's quarters, and on the master's desk, clipped and in a vase, was that rose. The gardener asked, "What in the world? You've clipped that white rose. I've cared for and nurtured that rose. Why have you cut it?" The master replied, "I thought you were tending it for me. I had a need, a use for that rose on my desk." The gardener understood.

In your life, God may have reached down and clipped a beautiful rose. But guess why He did it? In the death of that precious one, the Heavenly Father had a work and a purpose that could only be accomplished in that manner.

I think about two sons in the Bible. When Joseph's father, Jacob, came down into Egypt, Joseph showed much respect for him. He took him in to meet Pharaoh. He honored his father. What a testimony!

Then I think about Absalom. He broke his father's heart and defiled his father's house. Absalom died and children threw rocks at his burial place.

Which do you want to be? A Joseph or an Absalom? "Honor thy father and thy mother."

A man carried his wife and son to a lake area outside the city for a vacation. While the mother was fixing a meal in the house, the father and son went out on the lake in a boat for awhile. As sometimes occurs, a sudden storm came up, clouds covered the sun, and there was darkness all over the lake as the waves were billowing. Then the son and the father saw that the mother had put a light in the window, and the father said, "Son, I'm going to row. You keep your eyes on the light. Help me go in the direction of the light." They did and made it to the house safely. When they arrived home, the mother was there to greet them. The son said, "Mom, we came home safely because we steered by your light."

I wonder, when our children reach heaven, if they will come up to us and say, "Oh, Dad, oh, Mom, I made it home safe because I steered by your light."

6
The Sanctity of Life

(v. 13)

As we approach the Sixth Commandment, read verse 12 which is the Fifth Commandment. Then we will follow the flow of the Commandments right into verse 13.

> Honor thy father and they mother: that thy days may be long upon the land which the Lord thy God giveth thee. Thou shalt not kill.

In that statement, our God, for all time, established the sanctity of life.

President Bush, as he presented his 1991 Crime Bill, stated that the killings on the streets of our nation must stop now. He was emphasizing the thrust of this Commandment—"Thou shalt not kill."

In preparing this message, I decided I would closely watch the newspapers, listen to the news, and see where we are in America—and where we are in Jacksonville, Florida. Here are some of the horrors that have transpired this week.

A sailor was convicted of killing a mother and a daughter. He killed them both with a hammer. He attempted suicide two times this week. God says "Thou shalt not kill."

There is a new movie out about the drug-gang scene entitled *New Jack City*. It was shown in New York City, and a nineteen-year-old fellow was murdered. That movie is being shown right now in our city. God says "Thou shalt not kill."

A tearful mother testified before the Florida Legislature, pleading for them to enforce a policy that would keep a DUI offender in jail until he sobers up and that he not be released onto the streets until he "drys out." God says "Thou shalt not kill."

In Channelview, Texas, a mother hired a hit man to kill the

mother of another girl who was competing with her daughter for a slot as a cheerleader. God says "Thou shalt not kill."

In New Hampshire a seventeen-year-old boy, on his birthday, tearfully admitted the murder of the husband of his school-teacher. He killed him with a .38 handgun. He said in his testimony, "I wanted to be with Pam. That's what I had to do to be with Pam." Pam, the schoolteacher who talked him into killing her husband, testified that she didn't want him to kill her husband in front of her dog, lest her dog suffer psychological harm! God says "Thou shalt not kill."

There was also an account in the newspaper of a man who has been accused of murdering his own mother. God says "Thou shalt not kill."

The Senate Judiciary Committee declared that America has become the most violent, the most self-destructive nation on the earth. God says "Thou shalt not kill."

In this Commandment God has established the sanctity of human life. There are several reasons why this is such a serious crime. There are several reasons why God says "Thou shalt not kill." One reason is the *source of life*. The Bible teaches that God is the Giver of life. It is God alone who brings life into existence. There are two theories about the origin of life. There is the theory of creationism and the theory of evolution. If you believe in evolution, then that places mankind on a level no higher than animal life. If you believe in creationism, then you believe that every human life is precious in the sight of God, and that only God who gave life has the right to take life away. This is serious because God is the source of life.

It is also a serious crime because, once it is done, it cannot be undone. Some of these Commandments can be violated, and restitution can be made. For instance, The Eighth Commandment says "Thou shalt not steal." If you steal something from someone, most of the time you can make restitution and restoration. But if you take a human life it is impossible for you to give that life back again. Once the crime of murder is committed it can never, ever be undone.

We are dealing with the sanctity of human life. In many places human life means very little. We found that in the knowledge we gained of Saddam Hussein. We have discovered that he places very little value on human life, be it the lives of his enemies or the lives of his own people.

I remember reading about Napoleon Bonaparte who was making plans for a great battle. One of his associates said to him, "This will cost 100,000 of our men." He replied, "One hundred thousand men! What are 100,000 men to me?" Many people do not place much value on human life.

First of all, let us talk about:

What His Commandment Does Not Mean

It does not forbid the taking of animal life. In this same chapter (v. 24) God give instructions about burnt offerings and peace offerings of sheep and oxen. These animals were to be slain and laid on the altar. The Bible does teach humane treatment of animals. Proverbs 12:10 makes it clear that the righteous are to be concerned about the humane treatment of their animals.

Yet, the Bible has given us the right to kill animals for food. Genesis 9:3 says, "Every moving thing that liveth shall be meat for you; even as the green herb have I given you all things." Jesus ate fish. There is a qualitative difference between animal life and human life. In Genesis 2:7 where we are told about the creation of mankind, the Bible declares that God "breathed into his nostrils the breath of life, and man became a living soul." As far as I am able to find in Scripture, never is this phrase used —"the breath of life"—of any except human life. Only mankind has had breathed into it by God "the breath of life." The Bible states that we are made in the image of God. That is never spoken of animal life. The Bible further states that man is made after the likeness of God. Never is that written of animal life.

Neither does this Commandment forbid the declaration of war. You may remember that when President Bush was making plans to declare war in the Persian Gulf, he used the terminology "a just war." Those were carefully chosen words. Since the days of Saint Augustine and Thomas Aquinas the Christian church has developed the understanding of "a just war." The president was precisely following that concept. There are several matters involved. One, there must be a just cause in order to stop aggression in the world. Two, there must be a just intent in order to secure justice for all. Three, it must be waged only as a last resort when all other efforts have been exhausted. Four, it must also be declared by a legitimate authority. In other words, it recognizes that only established government has the right to declare war.

The Bible plainly teaches that there are some circumstances when war is just. If you should walk out of our church building, and one of our young women was attacked by a vicious thug—a violent criminal who was primed to kill her—wouldn't you go to her rescue? Wouldn't you feel some kind of responsibility to prevent the death of that precious person? If it is right to protect the innocent in those circumstances, it is also right to protect the innocent in broader circumstances. This commandment does not forbid the declaration of and the going to war—if such is just.

Neither does this Commandment forbid the death penalty. "Thou shalt not kill." The only one who has the right to snuff out life is the One who has given life. Therefore, only God has the authority to give people the right to take another life. God has done this in His word. In Genesis 9:6—"Whoso sheddeth man's blood, by man shall his blood be shed," for in the image of God made He man. So far as I am able to discover, that Commandment of God has never been revoked in Scripture. In Romans 13 it seems to be transparently clear that God grants legitimate government the authority to execute murderers. So, this does not forbid the taking of life in the death penalty. "Thou shalt not kill."

Now I want to share with you: What does it forbid?

What This Commandment Does Mean

The Outwardness of Killing

This refers to the outward act of killing. There are several kinds of killing I want to mention. One, of course is *homicide*, the taking of one human life by another human being. I read recently that 26,300 people are murdered in America every year. During each hour there will be three people killed in America—three people every hour, twenty-four hours a day, seven days a week, thirty days in the month, 365 days in the year. We are indeed living in a violent society.

I was in Atlanta, Georgia, for one day during the Persian Gulf War, en route to Alabama to preach that night. I read that day: during the same period of time during the Gulf War there were more people slain in Atlanta than Americans who die in the war. In other words, it was safer to be in Saudi Arabia or Kuwait than it was to be in the streets of Atlanta. God says "Thou shalt not kill." It is a crime against society; a crime against an individual; a crime against their families. It is a crime against the Holy God, who gave life, to take away life. So, there is *homicide*.

Then there is *suicide*. Suicide is taking one's own life. There are 30,000 suicides every year in the U.S. Some have estimated that there are as many as 400,000 attempted suicides every year. Suicide is becoming more and more an experience of young people. At least 5,000 young people a year succeed in taking their own lives. I have a personal conviction that in many instances of suicide, many are not mentally balanced at the time. I have even known believers in the Lord Jesus Christ, who in the times of intense duress, stress, or depression, have taken their own lives. So, many people are insane at the time of suicide. It is always a tragedy when it occurs. "I'm just going to take my own life. I'm just going to end it all." Suicide doesn't end it all, not for the family that is left with hurt and heartache that remains the rest of their lives. A person cannot avoid meeting God. It doesn't matter whether one dies of natural causes or unnatural causes, the Bible states "it is appointed unto men once to die, but after this the judgment" (Heb. 9:27). God is the only one who is good enough and wise enough and loving enough to know when it is time for your life here to end. There are no circumstances too unbearable that the God of heaven cannot help you pass through them and bring you to a deeper experience of His grace in spite of them. What a disaster when a person takes his own life!

There is another form of outward killing—*abortion*—the taking of the life of the unborn. In 1973 in Roe versus Wade, the Supreme Court declared that it was not against the law for a mother to abort her unborn baby. Since that time it is estimated almost 30,000,000 unborn babies have been killed in America. We are killing babies in America at the rate of a million and a half per year. That's 4,000 times every day an unborn baby loses its life. It is safer in this country—and there will be more protection by law—for snails in a river than for unborn babies in the wombs of their own mothers. It is a national disgrace and horror. I think it is the worst tragedy in the history of America. The killing of the unborn.

Somebody says, "Oh, Preacher, a woman has a right to her own body." I am not talking about the body of the mother. I am talking about the body of that baby. That unborn baby is not merely a mass of tissue, not merely an appendage that is tied on. The baby is a real life.

Did you know that the word *fetus* is Latin for *baby*? It is amazing and ironic that in many instances the very ones who demonstrate against the death penalty in front of prisons, where a convicted criminal is going to be executed, are, in some instances, the same people who stand outside abortion clinics and want to defend the "right" of a woman to snuff out the life of an innocent, unborn baby. That breaks my heart. I believe that life begins at conception, and I feel that is beyond debate. I do not think any reasonable person can argue with the truth that life begins at conception.

In 1967 the First International Conference on Abortion met in Washington, D.C. That was a quarter of a century ago. Sixty major authorities from medicine, ethics, law, and social sciences met together with only one dissenting vote. Here is the statement they made: "The majority of our group could find no point in time between the union of the sperm and the egg and the birth of the infant at which point we could say that fetus was not a human life. The changes occurring between implantation, a six-week embryo, a six-month fetus, a one-week-old child or a mature adult are merely stages of development and maturation." That is the statement of the scientific community.

There are certain data even more vital to me than the statements of the scientific community. The Bible teaches that the unborn baby is a person. When Jeremiah was discussing his own call from God, God said to the prophet (v. 1:5): "Before I formed thee in the belly, I knew thee. Before thou camest forth out of the womb, I sanctified thee, and I ordained thee a prophet unto the nations." Have you read Psalm 139 lately? That is one of the most beautiful statements about the life of the unborn anywhere recorded in literature.

Psalm 139:13–16:

> For thou hast possessed my reins [this is as if the unborn baby were talking], thou hast covered me in my mother's womb. I will praise thee; for I am fearfully and wonderfully made: Marvelous

are thy works; and that my soul knoweth right well. My substance [bony framework] was not hid from thee, when I was made in secret, and curiously wrought in the lowest parts of the earth. Thine eyes did see thy substance [embryo] yet being unperfect; and in thy book all my members were written.

In the New Testament there are two basic words used for a child. One is the Greek word, *teknon*. It is the word routinely used in 1 John where John writes, "My little children" (2:1). It emphasizes the relationship between parent and child. There is another word in Greek for baby—*brephos*. When the Lord Jesus was born and the angels appeared to the shepherds, those angels instructed the shepherds (Luke 2:12): "Ye shall find the babe wrapped in swaddling clothes, lying in a manger." It is this word *brephos*. Jesus had already been born. He was then in a manger, and the message from heaven was, you will find the *brephos* in a manger.

That word occurs eight times in the Greek New Testament. Six times it refers to a baby that has already been born. The other two times it appears in Luke 1.

There is also the account of the birth of John the Baptist who was "forerunner" of the Lord Jesus. When Mary discovered she was going to give birth to the Savior she went to the hill country to visit Elisabeth, her cousin, and announced she was going to give birth. Elisabeth was "great with child"—expecting John. Verse 41—"And it came to pass, that, when Elisabeth heard the salutation of Mary, the baby [*brephos*] leaped in her womb." Verse 44—"For, lo, as soon as the voice of thy salutation sounded in mine ears, the baby [*brephos*] leaped in my womb for joy." God, beyond question, teaches that the unborn baby in the womb of its mother is a real human life, and God says "Thou shalt not kill."

Follow me for awhile in the journey of an unborn baby. At seventeen days the unborn baby has new life in its own blood cells. At eighteen days the unborn baby has pulsation, which begins what will ultimately will be the heart. At nineteen days the eyes start to develop. At twenty days the foundation of the entire nervous system is laid down. At twenty-four days the heart has regular beats. At twenty-eight days the arms and legs are forming. You can place an object in its hand and it will grasp it. It can swim, kick, and turn somersaults.

In thirty days regular blood flow and a vascular system are there.

Eyes and nasal development have begun. At forty days the heart energy output is 20 percent of that of an adult. At forty-two days the skeleton is complete. Reflexes are present. At forty-three days brain-wave patterns can be recorded. That is normally ample evidence that thinking is taking place. At forty-nine days the baby appears as a miniature doll; at seven weeks with fingers and toes. At eight weeks, all the organs are functioning. Kidneys, liver, brain— all systems are intact.

All future growth develops from what is present at eight weeks. At nine or ten weeks, the baby squints, swallows, and sticks out its tongue. At eleven or twelve weeks, arms and legs begin to move. At sixteen weeks, sexual organs are differentiated. At eighteen weeks, vocal chords are working, the baby can cry. At twenty weeks, hair is on the head. The baby ordinarily will weigh approximately one pound—all of that in a twenty-week period of time. God says "Thou shalt not kill."

Here are five reasons why abortion is killing.

1. The victim is unquestionably innocent.
2. The victim is helpless.
3. The order to kill comes from the victim's own mother.
4. It is always a reasoned, calculated, intentional act. At least that's what the abortion clinics claim. They tell us they always carefully counsel the mother about what they are about to do.
5. Abortion is paid killing—a business transaction.

If I went into detail on the process of abortion in this book, it would offend you. For many, it would be physically sickening. The head is crushed, the body is mutilated. Or, if saline solution is used, it burns and poisons the baby's body on the inside. God says "Thou shalt not kill."

Taking life by murder, suicide, or abortion, violates the Commandment of God. There is not only direct murder, but there is indirect killing. Not only is there primary killing, but there is secondary killing. By that I mean you can kill indirectly. You can kill by hiring a hit man, as the mother did in Texas who wanted her girl to be elected cheerleader. King David did that. He saw to it that someone else killed Uriah so David might cover his sin. You can do it indirectly by drunken driving, guilty of murder by drunken driving. Half of the traffic deaths by accident in this country are a result of DUI. Forty-five thousand people a year are killed—slaughtered on our streets by drunken driving. Half of the traffic deaths by accident in this country are a result of DUI. Forty-five thousand people a year are killed—slaughtered on our streets by drunken driving. The sale of alcoholic beverages is indirect killing. One may rationalize it however one may wish; alcohol has many defenders but no defense. You can't get around it. In 50 to 80 percent of all murders, alcohol is involved. In 30 percent of all suicides, alcohol is involved. The Bible has pronounced a curse upon all of those who have anything to do with the legalization, sale, use, or the buying of alcoholic beverages.

The Book of Habakkuk says, "Woe to him that buildeth a town with blood, and stablisheth a city by iniquity!" (2:12). "Woe unto him that giveth his neighbor drink, that putteth thy bottle to him, and makest him drunken also, that thou mayest look on their nakedness" (v. 15). Over every lounge in this city it should be written "Thou shalt not kill." Over every liquor store in this city it should be proclaimed: "Thou shalt not kill." Over every club that sells liquor in this city a big sign should be placed: "Thou shalt not kill." I hate liquor with every fiber of my being. I'm against liquor. If I had one little toe, and it wiggled toward liquor—I'd chop it off. That's how I hate liquor. It is a form of indirect killing.

Other narcotics are involved—cocaine, heroin, uppers,downers, all types of "dope." It is estimated that thousands of murders are committed per year because of dope. Many addicts will kill for a "fix"—a snort of cocaine, a shot of heroin, a Quaalude, you name it. Many countries make the sale of drugs punishable by death. America's escalating crime rate is directly linked to alcohol and other drugs.

You can kill people by other ways, too. You can kill a reputation. By your whispering criticisms you can slay a reputation. By unjust, unkind statements, one can kill the testimony of some Christian brother. I know some boys and girls who are killing their parents in slow motion.

A son was breaking the heart of his mother by his wicked, wayward life. The father in exasperation asked, "Why don't you just take a gun and go up to Mother's bedroom and kill her now? It would be a mercy for you to kill her now than for you to kill her by slow motion with the life you are living."

How many mates kill one another by slow degrees of unlove. How many families are killed by insulting remarks and by unkind words spoken in anger, bitterness, and insensitivity? God says "Thou shalt not kill."

So far, you say, "I'm all right. I'm not guilty of violating this Commandment."

The Inwardness of Killing

You can violate this Commandment and never go to jail or serve one day of your term. You can violate this Commandment, and it may never be seen. Our Lord Jesus stressed these Ten Commandments and showed us the inwardness of them.

In Mark 7 our Lord Jesus treats the inwardness of sin. He shows us that all sin originates not in the outward act, but in the inward attitude. So in verses 20–21 He observes, "That which cometh out of the man, that defileth the man. For from within out of the heart of men, proceed evil thoughts, adulteries, fornications, murders." Jesus tracks the monster of murder back to its cage. He declares it all starts in the human heart. One's heart, apart from the grace of God, is capable of every sin that anybody has ever committed on this earth. The seeds of killing are in every human heart.

In Matthew 5:21–22, the Sermon on the Mount, is our Lord's sermon about this Commandment. "You have heard that it was said by them of old time, Thou shalt not kill; and whosoever shall kill shall be in danger of the judgment: But I say unto you, That whosoever is angry with his brother without a cause shall be in danger of the judgment: and whosoever shall say to his brother, Raca, shall be in danger of the council: but whosoever shall say, Thou fool shall be in danger of hell fire." Jesus taught that the crime of murder starts, first of all, with thinking, with anger in the heart.

Do you have anger in your heart toward someone? There is legitimate anger. The Bible says "Be ye angry and sin not." But there is an illegitimate anger. The Bible also says "let not the sun go down upon thy wrath" (Eph. 4:26). Anger nourished in the heart, anger fermented in the heart, easily turns to hate. It is the prelude to murder before the outward act. Be careful about that anger and how you handle that anger. It starts with thinking. It moves to talking—what people say expresses their anger, and the next step is the deed. It all starts down in the human heart—the inwardness of killing.

The Forgiveness of Killing

God condemns this violation, and the Bible makes it clear in the Book of Revelation that the murderer shall not inherit eternal life. But the murderer shall have his place in the lake of fire. "Preacher, that's a hard word, to know that killing is condemned." There may be a woman who has had an abortion. She may feel bad about it. She is grieving about it and feels so guilty about it. I have good news for her. She ought to thank God she feels guilty. She ought to thank God she is grieving about it. Grief is an expression of sorrow. Guilt is an expression of sin. That means there is hope for her. If she had been guilty of killing an unborn baby, I have good news. God hates her sin, but God loves her. God will forgive her. Jesus died on the cross for her sin. Jesus shed His blood for her sin.

I received a letter from a man on death row in prison. He wrote that he felt I was rather hard on the murderers. He testified he had been saved, thank God. What about the murderer himself and compassion for the murderer? I do have compassion for the murderer. I have good news for you, too, if you have been guilty of murder. If you were convicted of it, it doesn't mean that there is no more penalty attached to it. You may escape the bar of human justice, but you will not escape the bar of God's justice. The very blood of your victim(s) will cry out of the earth. But I want that man on death row to realize that God can forgive him.

Would you agree with me that three of the greatest men in the Bible are Moses, David, and Paul? Do you recall that Moses was guilty of killing an Egyptian? David was guilty of the killing of Uriah. Paul was guilty of killing Christians. Yet look at your Bible. The first five books of the Bible were written by Moses. Most of the Psalms, the longest book in the Bible, were composed by David. Perhaps half of the New Testament was written by Paul. Murderers all, but who had been saved by the grace of God. I have good news for you. You can be saved, and you can be forgiven. When Jesus Christ was preparing to go to the cross, Pontius Pilate presented Barabbas and Jesus to the crowd. Barabbas was in jail partly because of murder. The Lord Jesus Christ, the Son of God, knew no sin. Neither was there any guile in His mouth. The question was, "Which one do you want to release?" The crowd screamed for the release of Barabbas, but for Jesus' death.

Perhaps you will remark, "I've had it pretty easy in this message. I've never violated this Commandment. I've never killed anybody directly or indirectly." I have a sad retort for you. You are guilty of the greatest murder ever committed on this earth. In Act 3:14–15 the apostle Peter was preaching shortly after the crucifixion of Jesus. "But ye denied the Holy One and the Just [Jesus], and desired a murderer [Barabbas] to be granted unto you; And killed the Prince of life." You are not only guilty of homicide. You are guilty of *deicide*. You are guilty of the death of God's dear Son, the Lord Jesus Christ. It was your hands and mine that drove the nails into His hands. It was our hard hearts that plaited the crown of thorns and pressed them upon His brow. It was our wicked souls that thrust the spear into His side. We are guilty of the worst killing ever perpetrated—the killing of the lovely Son of God, Jesus Himself.

I have good news for you. God will forgive you. God will cleanse you and save you. Jesus died for you and me. He shed His blood that we might be forgiven of our sins.

7
"Safe Sex"
(v. 14)

The 1631 edition of the *King James Version* came to be known as "The Wicked Bible." It seems that when the printers were preparing to print that particular edition, an error was made, and one word was left out of verse 14. The word *not* was not included in that edition, and it read, "Thou shalt commit adultery."

On the basis of contemporary sexual morals it seems that many people prefer the edition of "The Wicked Bible." We seem to be living in an atmosphere when this Commandment of God is more disregarded and belittled than perhaps at any other time in history. The Seventh Commandment is the Creator's law which guards the chastity of marriage, the sanctity of the family, and the preservation of society. Violation of this Commandment of God has been a source of broken homes; it has been a source of wrecked lives; it has been a source of disease and even death.

We are living in a day which has experienced the "sexual revolution." It really started back in the 1960s or before, and has continued to our day. Everywhere there seems to be a total assault on this Commandment of God. God says, "Thou shalt not commit adultery." But people have scorned, ridiculed, and belittled this Commandment. We see it in the area of entertainment. Comedians ridicule this Commandment. Movies and television make sexual immorality a common occurrence. Very rarely on television are lovers husband and wife in a marriage relationship. It seems they are always outside the relationship of marriage. By means of camera angles and makeup, they create images of people that do not exist. Viewers are given a warped view of what sexuality and sexual fulfillment are all about.

There is also an attack in the area of advertisement. Advertisers have discovered that sex sells. Sex is used to sell anything from beer to toothpaste to cereal. We also note that alcohol and drugs are contributing factors against God's command concerning sexual purity. By the means of alcohol and/or other drugs, many attempt to lower inhibitions and standards so people will do things under the influence of alcohol they would never do otherwise. Also, ours is the day of the "Playboy philosophy." We have been influenced largely in American society by this concept which claims that sex is a normal function of the body. It is a desire which mankind shares with animals, like sleeping or eating. Therefore, it is only natural to satisfy these normal desires. So, the playboy claims that we should throw off all of our inhibitions, find a partner of like mind, and enter into a "meaningful relationship."

Let me share a shocker with you. Josh McDowell has done extensive studies of Christian young people in the area of sexual morality. He has found that even among evangelical church young people in America, 65 percent claim they have had some sexual experience before the age of eighteen. Forty-three percent point out they have had sexual intercourse before the age of eighteen. Keep in mind that this same survey reports that young people in the average church learn their morals concerning sex from movies. Seventy-three percent say they receive little or no direction from their church. Here is the good news in all of that. Dr. McDowell found that young people who keep sexually pure do so on the basis of a born-again experience with Jesus Christ and a commitment to the Bible, God's Holy Word.

That's why in the youth ministry of our church we place emphasis on what God teaches about this matter of sexual purity. We teach our young people where the moral fences are, why those fences are there, and why they ought to stay within God's guidelines and direction in this matter. We are living now in an age when the word *sex* is associated with words like *perversion, prostitution, VD,* and *AIDS.* It ought to be associated with beautiful words like *marriage, home, love,* and *babies.*

Now the emphasis is on "safe sex." Society has discovered that there are certain penalties attached to sexual immorality. But rather than coming back to God's standard and obeying His laws concerning sexual morality, our society cries out "safe sex" in public schools, in magazines and newspapers, and in public-service commercials on TV and radio.

I want to talk to you about "safe sex" according to God's Word. There are three words I will use in pulling from this commandment of God the genuine meaning there.

Sexuality

Focus on this undergirding statement of God, "Thou shalt not commit adultery." Underlying that is the word, *sexuality.* According to the Bible the origin of sexuality is in God Himself. Our generation did not invent sex. Of course, we are not the first generation that has discovered the reality of sex. The gift of sex was presented by God. In the Book of Genesis, after God created the universe and then created man, the Word says that God "created them male and female." There is nothing dirty about sex, nothing ugly about it. Hebrews 13:4 says, "Marriage is honorable in all, and the bed undefiled." That's God's statement about the sanctity of sex.

Sexual identity is clearly commanded by God. Whatever Deuteronomy 22:5, that has to do with the apparel of men and women, and 1 Corinthians 11:14–15, that has to do with the hairstyles of men and women, may teach, it certainly is evident that both have a message about the importance of maintaining sexual identity. The Bible teaches that a man ought to look like a man; a woman ought to look like a woman. Any blurring of sexual distinctions is disobedience to the teaching of God's Word.

It is important that we teach God's view of sexual conduct and identity in our churches. We have new converts, "babes in Christ," coming into our churches. Many of these new Christians coming in have no background whatsoever. Some have seldom, if ever, been inside a church, and do not know what church is all about. They look to us who are older and more mature as their role models and guides. I want to thank godly men and women who teach our young converts the importance of modest apparel and what is proper to be worn in certain places. My wife, Janet, has always been a perfect lady. Ladies, you could follow her life-style and her apparel, and you would never go wrong. We are in a day when it is often impossible to tell who is male and who is female from clothes, hairstyles, and actions!

The fact that God originated sex also means that there is a spiritual dimension to it. If you leave out the spiritual aspect of sex, you lower it to the animal level. Sexuality, then, descends to the level of the barnyard, and a person becomes perceived not as a person, but a thing, an object, a body to be used, a mass of flesh to be taken advantage of. Thus, a person with divinely intended sexuality is then debased and devoid of importance and worth. This Commandment also indicates the intention of sexuality.

God has intended that His glorious gift of sex be placed in a particular circle. The Bible's intention is that there be one man, one woman in one marriage. The sexual relationship is to occur within the circle of marriage. That is the intention of God. Within that circle the sexual experience is beautiful, meaningful, and fulfilling. I think there are two primary purposes for sexual intercourse in marriage. One is for the propagation of the race. The Bible teaches in the Book of Genesis that God commanded the man and the woman, "Multiply, and replenish the earth" (1:28). A husband and a wife share with God in the creation of human life. Another reason for the sexual experience in marriage is for mutual fulfill-ment. In Ecclesiastes 9:9 the Bible says, "Live joyfully with the wife whom thou lovest all the days of the life of thy vanity." There is mutual fulfillment in the marriage experience.

Some question the entire area of sexual experience in marriage and raise the question of abstinence. Turn to 1 Corinthians 7:1. I want to show you God's statement concerning the value of the sexual relationship in a marriage. "Now concerning the things whereof ye wrote unto me: It is good for a man not to touch a woman." Paul is teaching to keep oneself pure before marriage. "Nevertheless to avoid fornication, let every man have his own wife and let every woman have her own husband. Let the husband render unto the wife due benevolence [let the husband give to the wife her due—that is, he gives himself sexually to her]: and like-wise also the wife [gives herself sexually] unto the husband. The wife hath not power of her own body, but the husband: and likewise the husband hath not power of his own body, but the wife. Defraud ye not one the other, except it be with consent for a time, that you may give yourselves to fasting and prayer; and come together again, that Satan tempt you not for your incontinency [lack of self-control]" (vv. 2–5).

This passage does not extol the virtues of abstinence. This passage is not in the Bible to encourage you to see how long in your marriage you can do without sex. This passage of Scripture is a statement that warns of the dangers of sexual abstinence. There may be valid reasons why a husband and wife may not come together on certain occasions. Some are health reasons; others are because of fasting and prayer as given in this passage. I want to make it very clear—it is not a sign of special spirituality that you are able to withhold sex from each other for an extended period of time. That is not an evidence of spiritual depth. You have to make a difference between that which is sinful and that which is not wise. There is a difference between those two. To see how long a married couple can do without sex is not a sign of spiritualty—it is a sign of immaturity. So, within the circle of marriage God encourages sexual relationships between the husband and the wife. God says, "Thou shalt not commit adultery." That Commandment has to do with sexuality.

Here's the second word I want to lay on our heart. This commandment has to do with:

Immorality

You could read the Commandment this way, and it would be crystal clear—"Thou shalt not commit immorality." That is God's law concerning sexual purity. Of course, none of us like rules. We immediately rebel when we see them. That's one of the underlying premises of Paul's teaching in the Book of Romans. It is that the flesh naturally recoils from rules. If you are walking down the street and see a sign that reads, "Don't walk on the grass," what do you want to do? Walk on the grass. Or you see a sign that says, "Don't look under this lid." You want to pull up the lid and look in. Yet, you and I recognize that rules are absolutely essential. You can't play any kind of game without rules. When everybody does what he wants to do in a game, if there are no boundary lines, no regulations, then the game collapses.

The same situation is true in other areas of life. You must have rules, guidelines, restrictions. So, God makes this prohibition, "Thou shalt not commit immorality." God's Word is unmistakable about this in Scripture. There are several passages in the Old Testament where the penalty for the violation of God's law concerning sexual purity was death. Hebrews 13:4 says "Marriage is honorable in all, and the bed undefiled; but whoremongers and adulterers God will judge." It is a serious sin that God will judge.

How is this sin committed? There are two primary ways. First of all, there is *physical immorality*. When you consider the teachings of the Lord Jesus in the New Testament, you will find that an additional word is added to the Old Testament statement of *adultery*. You will also encounter *fornication*. Jesus in Matthew 15 refers to what springs from the heart. "Those things which proceed out of the mouth come forth from the heart . . . adulteries, fornication" (vv. 18–19). Then in the Book of Galatians, Paul writes about "the works of the flesh." He mentions *adultery* and *fornication*. Those two words explain how sexual immorality can be committed in a physical manner. Turn to 1 Thessalonians 4 and read about the first way you can commit sexual immorality. That is by fornication, which is premarital sex. "For this is the will of God, even your sanctification, that ye should abstain from fornication: That everyone of you should know how to possess his vessel [how to acquire your wife] in sanctification and honor: Not in the lust of concupiscence [personal desire], even as the Gentiles which know not God" (vv. 3–5).

When an unmarried person commits the sexual act with another person they are guilty of the sin of premarital immorality. It is so common today that it is a tragedy. God has not changed His law. It doesn't matter what the "standards" are today. It doesn't matter if everybody else is going in the wrong direction. Merely because people choose not to believe doesn't negate God's laws. Oh, the heartache of people who commit the sin of sexual immorality.

Let me present some reasons why it is wrong to commit fornication and why premarital sex is a sin. Number one, it is an act that is usually done in secret—in the backseat of a car or in an out-of-the-way, hidden place. Rather than being beautiful, sacred, and pure, it becomes an act dragged into the dark corners and hiding places. That is one reason not to do it.

Number two, it invariably causes fear and guilt. One major university several years ago did a survey of the young ladies on its campus. The survey revealed that there is a direct correlation between sexual immorality and personal emotional problems. It takes its toll on a person—stress, fear, guilt. So, don't commit fornication—it can ruin your life. It hinders your chances of a happy marriage later. Another university did a study of young men. They discovered that young men who are sexually active before marriage are a poor risk for a long-lasting marital relationship. There is a characteristic about committing this sin that causes an individual to lose respect for the value and worth of other people.

Young ladies, that guy who is pushing you to lower your sexual standards in order to "prove your love" for him is a selfish jerk. The next time a fellow says, "If you love me, you'd prove it to me," you tell junior to pack his diapers and head back home to momma. If this happens and you yield, more often than not he will drop you like a hot potato, and your name will become kind of like a dirty old ball that's bounced around in the locker rooms at school. Your name can become a common commodity around the school, and it will greatly hinder your chances of a happy marriage.

Here's another reason why you ought not to commit fornication. When you've gone "all the way," you really haven't gone all the way. You think when you've committed the sex act you have gone all the way. There's that silent ride home in a guilt-filled car. There is that uncomfortable feeling when you reach home, your mom and dad see you then or later, and you have all that guilt down in your soul. You haven't gone all the way when you commit immorality. You have to face your parents, your friends, and others. You haven't gone all the way because then come those nervous days when you make up your mind never to do that again. A while later, you may do it again. No, you haven't gone all the way. Then there may be those terrifying weeks when you are afraid you may be pregnant. You may be wondering, *Am I pregnant? Am I going to have to tell my family I'm pregnant?* You haven't gone all the way until you may marry that boy. Then in the first fuss you have he throws your sexual immorality in your face—then you've gone all the way. Premarital sex is wrong. Why? Because God says so, first of all. "Thou shalt not commit immorality."

The other word *adultery* has to do with extramarital sex, sex outside the established circle of marriage. For years that has been called an affair. That seems to be the theme song of the average television program and movie today. Such behavior is magnified and exalted. Many are teaching that a little sexual immorality on the side is not bad. Even certain humanistic psychologists and psychiatrists claim it would be good for some couples to have a "little affair." That's like claiming it might be good to put a "little match" in a gunpowder factory. Such thinking is dangerous.

If we live long enough, we will reach the mid-life crisis. Men reach that point and wonder, "Have I still got it? Can I attract a younger person?" People laugh about it. I was on an airplane a few years ago, and several businessmen were bragging about their extramarital affairs and sexual exploits. They were really "macho." Sir, you're not macho when you cheat on your wife. You are the sorriest piece of plunder on this earth. Hopefully, you have a sweet wife who loves you. You may have boys and girls at home who trust you and are counting on you. God have mercy on your soul. God forbids sexual immorality—extramarital sex.

The first reason is because such a relationship is built on getting instead of giving. The sexual experience is one of the most giving acts a person can perform. You should give yourself completely as an expression of your love for an individual, but an affair involves trying to *get*. It can never be ultimately satisfying because it is based on guilt rather than trust. A relationship, to last, has to be based on trust. If you have an affair on the side, and wind up marrying the other person, how are you ever going to have any trust? God asserts, "Thou shalt not commit immorality." You can commit it by physical immorality.

There's another way one can commit this sin—*mental immorality.* You can commit it in your mind. Note the Sermon on the Mount in Matthew 5. Here is the commentary of our Savior on the Seventh Commandment, "Thou shalt not commit immorality." Jesus goes deeper than the letter of the law, down beneath the surface of the physical act. In verses 27–28 Jesus said, "Ye have heard that it was said by them of old time, Thou shalt not commit adultery. But I say unto you, That whosoever looketh on a woman to lust after her hath committed adultery with her already in his heart." Jesus was referring to mental immorality. He was not thinking of the first look, the involuntary glance. The wording of the language means a deliberate stare. It means that second look with intended lust on the mind.

Look at 2 Peter 2:14—"Having eyes full of adultery, and that cannot cease from sin." Right there in the Word of God is one of the most vivid statements concerning "sexual addiction" to be found anywhere. "Sexual addiction." We haven't heard that terminology until recent times. The Word of God lays it before us. "Having eyes full of adultery, that cannot cease from sin."

Psychologists have identified three levels of sexual addiction. It all starts exactly where Jesus pinpointed it—in one's thought life. Level one of sexual addiction falls into these areas—pornography and all kinds of fantasies. Many Christians have a secret thought life. Nobody else but God knows about it. Many minds are sewers and not sanctuaries. Many men and women are relishing thoughts of immorality in their minds. They sit in their dens, and television and videos pump scene after scene of sexual immorality into their own homes. Or they pick up pornographic magazines when no other person knows, when they are in secret. Men and women begin to feed their thought life on pornography. Men can become addicted, but so can women who more often read so-called "romances" or certain women's magazines. Or, they begin to look at members of the opposite sex with lust. People have certain barriers in their minds that keep it a secret mental affair. They don't want their wife, husband, children, or their fellow Christians to know. Those are social barriers that become dikes in the mind that keep the sea of mental immorality from bursting out into our lives.

But be careful, Sir, you may be filling up the level of your thought life. Your eyes may be focused on adultery. I also speak to women. You are beginning to let the level of your sexual fantasies become more and more intense. Then, psychologists ascertain, you move to level two. That is when you begin to become bold in your sexual fantasies. Some begin to act out their fantasies outwardly. Men often move into the areas of voyeurism, indecent exposure, or seeking out a prostitute.

A detective in our sheriff's department told me there are 700 known prostitutes in Jacksonville. Eighty of them have known cases of AIDS. Level two—sexual addiction—if you keep on doing what Jesus forbade us to do, looking with lust in one's heart, then one breaks down the barriers, the dikes start crumbling and one moves into level two. Then a man may start finding prostitutes and becoming involved more deeply. If it keeps on going—the Scriptures says they "cannot cease from sin"—they are hooked. They are addicted to sexual immorality—sexual perversion. Then it moves into level three—rape, consorting with a prostitute, affairs, deviant behavior.

He was brought up in what, he himself said, was a good family. His parents were solid loving parents. He was active in the youth group in his church. A grandfather had introduced him to pornographic books. He began to read the pornography and feed his thought life on it. As that kind of stuff progressed, there came a time when the soft-core porn didn't provide the sort of sexual stimulation he was seeking, so he moved into the hard core. Then that didn't suit him, so he began seeking out prostitutes. Then that wasn't satisfying, and he began to rape. Finally, that didn't produce the sexual thrills he was thirsting for, and he started killing and mutilating helpless girls. That man was Ted Bundy, executed in Florida. "Eyes full of adultery, that cannot cease from sin."

Many Christians have a secret thought life. I warn you: deal decisively with that situation in your life, or you are headed for terrible heartache down the road.

In Matthew 5:28 Jesus teaches about mental immorality. Now look at verses 29 and 30. "If thy right eye offend thee, pluck it out, and cast it from thee: for it is profitable for thee that one of thy members should perish, and not that they whole body should be cast into hell. If they right hand offend thee, cut it off, and cast if from thee: for it is profitable for thee that one of thy members should perish, and not that thy whole body should be cast into hell." Is Jesus suggesting literally you ought to pull out a knife and cut off a hand? The text is plain that the problem is not in the eye—it's in the heart. The problem is not with the hand but with the heart. Jesus demands that we deal quickly, decisively, and severely by radical spiritual surgery with anything that is leading a person in the direction of sexual impurity. Rather than plucking out your eye, cancel your *Playboy* or *Cosmopolitan* subscription. Rather than cutting off your hand, cancel sex-slanted cable television. Walk away from places that would cause you to head in the wrong direction. Throw out trashy books, records, cassettes, videos. Stop frequenting places that would cause you to be guilty of mental immorality. Mental immorality is the first step toward physical immorality.

This Commandment has to do with sexuality; it has to do with immorality; it has to do with:

Purity

Every one of these Commandments cast in a negative mode can also be read in a positive manner. The Commandment which says "Thou shalt not commit immorality" is also positive because it indicates, "Thou shalt be pure." This Commandment has to do with purity. You ought to commit yourself to sexual purity for several reasons. Number one, you ought to do it for *national reasons.* No nation can survive a collapse of sexual morals. The late Pitirim Sorokin of Harvard University, in his book entitled *The American Revolution*, wrote, "Unless there is a change in America we are doomed for the ash heap. No civilization, no nation, no empire has survived obsession with sex and impurity. This disease is eating the heart out of America." God's judgment is on the sin of sexual immorality. AIDS, prostitution, all of these sexual catastrophes are not an indication God's judgment is coming on America. Rather, it is an indication judgment is already here! So, for the sake of our nation we ought to keep ourselves pure. We ought to take our stand against pornography all over this country. We ought to protest those stores that sell pornography; we ought to call television stations when their programs are sexually offensive; we ought to oppose any legislation that would legitimize perverted sex styles in this country. All over this nation there is pending or passed legislation that would make it possible for homosexuals to adopt children. Christians ought to oppose these trends in our states and in our nation. Keep yourself pure for national reasons.

Keep yourself pure for *marital reasons.* You owe it to yourself to enter your marriage with purity. You owe it to your marriage, if you are already married, to keep your marriage pure. We are living in a generation that claims to know more about sex than any other. The truth of the matter is this generation understands about as little as any generation. Our generation talks about "making love." They call the culmination of the marriage experience making love. That's not making love—it's *expressing* love. Make up your mind you are going to keep purity in your marriage.

You can do that with several approaches—*cultivate love.* Ephesians 5:25 says, "Husbands, love your wives." Wives, love your husbands. Spouses often comment, "I don't love my husband anymore." "I don't love my wife anymore." You are not going to gain sympathy from me out of that. God *commands* you to love your husband or wife. It's a matter of your obedience or disobedience. Love is not an emotion that sweeps over you like a spell. We often think it does. Our songs are written like that—like it's going to infect you like the hives—all of a sudden you have "it," and you are itching all over.

No. *Love is a choice.* Love is not a diamond you discover. Love is more like a fragile flower that you cultivate, nourish, and protect. You have to work at cultivating it. You wives have to work on keeping romance in your marriage. Remember how you used to dress and primp when you were dating that old boy. Now he comes home, and you have your ten-year-old bathrobe on. You wear sandals or bedroom shoes that don't match. You have hardware in your hair. You have meringue all over your face. To be perfectly honest with you guys, most of us men have all the finesse of an eighteen-wheeler. So husbands and wives have to cultivate it.

The story goes that Eve asked, "Adam, do you love me?" He looked around and replied, "Who else?" He could honestly answered, "You are the only girl in the world for me." You have to work at it. Keep pornography out of your home. Keep sorry, filthy movies out of your home. Commit yourself to *marital purity.*

Commit yourself to *personal purity.* Make up your mind you are going to be sexually pure. You will be so thankful you did. You will be thrilled you obeyed God's Commandment and kept yourself sexually pure. It will work wonders for you emotionally and spiritually.

Perhaps you might remark, "Preacher, it's too late for me. I didn't get your sermon in time. I've already been guilty of the sin of immorality." We have a Savior who can take all the broken pieces of your home and your heart, if you will give them to Him, and He can put them back together.

There are certain people, unfortunately, who seem to assume the approach that, if you have been guilty of the sin of adultery, fornication, or immorality, you can never again be clean. But what God has cleansed, do not call unclean. In John 8:3–11 we see the woman "taken in adultery" who was brought to Jesus. I have always wondered where the man was. The law was clear. They were correct on the law. The law said she was to be stoned to death. Jesus said, "He that is without sin among you, let him first cast a stone." (v. 7). I heard a black preacher declare, "If a one of them dared to throw a rock at her, the Lord would have turned the heart of it to rubber, and it would have bounced back and burst their brains out." "He that is without sin among you let him first cast a stone." You can almost hear the thud of the rocks falling as they lined up, the oldest first, and filed away. Then Jesus said, "Woman, where are those thine accusers? Hath no man condemned thee? She said, No man, Lord. And Jesus said, unto her . . . go, and sin no more." (vv. 10–11).

8
Respect Other People's Property

(v. 15)

Talk about the timing of the Lord. He has arranged it so we will be studying the Commandment, "Thou shalt not steal," the night before April 15—the Internal Revenue deadline! Don't try to tell me the Lord doesn't have a sense of humor.

When I came in I saw several people with gloomy expressions on their faces. With some it is because they have to put that check in the mail tomorrow. If your ship ever does come in, IRS will be there to help you unload it!

I heard about a person who wrote to the IRS and said, "My conscience is bothering me. I owe you some money that I have not paid. Here is a check for $100. P. S. if I still can't sleep I'll send the rest of it." We'll send all we can tomorrow so we will be able to go to sleep.

These three Commandments of God are sort of tied together. With "Thou shalt not kill," "Thou shalt not commit adultery," "Thou shalt not steal," God is safeguarding issues vital to life. The Sixth Commandment safeguards life because God says "Thou shalt not kill." The Seventh Commandment safeguards marriage and the family because God says, "Thou shalt not commit adultery." This Eighth Commandment safeguards property, for God states, "Thou shalt not steal." These Commandments give us the basic building blocks of a moral society. In *Time* magazine (January, 1990), America's most renowned child psychiatrist, Robert Coles of Harvard University, commented on the fact that, in many of our nation's schools, we have rejected spiritual values. "This is one of the great problems in American public schooling," Coles wrote. "The teachers are afraid to bring up moral, let alone spiritual questions, for fear that they are going to violate the Constitution. It's a tragedy intellectually as well as morally and spiritually. . . . Children should be taught history that connects with their actual history, namely the history of the great religions, what those religions have been about, culturally, aesthetically, intellectually, morally, and spiritually. That learning could reform the moral lives of those children and classroom life."

We have many Christian people in the public school system—splendid administrators and devoted classroom teachers, but the system in which they must operate makes it difficult for them to teach moral values because you simply cannot separate morality from religion. You cannot teach morality well when you cannot nail the Ten Commandments on the wall of a schoolroom in America. It is a tremendous challenge today, but I believe that one of these days in God's grace, the pendulum is going to swing back, and we are going to return the Bible and prayer to our public schools, making it possible once again for us to teach the foundational building blocks upon which a substantial national morality can be taught. God says, "Thou shalt not steal."

On the surface this Commandment seems very simple. All of us know what stealing is. Stealing is taking something which does not belong to us, but as you plunge deeper into the subject you discover that it is far more serious than this. For instance, I found, in preparation for this message, some synonyms for "steal" in the dictionary: *extort, seize, burglarize, defraud, filch, heist, cheat, beguile, bilk, misappropriate, chisel, pilfer, pillage, plunder, rob, snitch, swindle, swipe, fleece, filmflam, gyp, sham, embezzle, bamboozle.* So we are dealing with a subject that is far more complicated than we may think.

The Universal Almanac of 1990 published statistics of crime in America for the year 1987. Burglaries (theft of property) numbered more than 12 million in 1987. In a ten-year period since 1978 that was a 19 percent increase in property crime in America. It is estimated that these goods were worth about 11.8 billion dollars stolen that year.

Every year in America we are experiencing more and more theft—people taking that which does not belong to them. The Bible says, "Thou shalt not steal." When God gives a Commandment, to violate that Commandment is an extremely serious matter. In fact, in 2

Corinthians 6:10 the Bible says that a thief will not inherit the kingdom of God. So, a person cannot go to heaven unless he is saved from the sin of stealing. The Bible warns about the seriousness of stealing in the life of a person after he is saved. Ephesians 4:28 says, "Let him that stole, steal no more, but rather let him labor." Some people have rephrased and repunctuated it, and read it this way: "Let him that stole, steal, no more let him labor." That's not how God wrote it in the Bible. God said "Let [them who] stole steal no more" because God said "Thou shalt not steal." I want to share with you certain truths God has incorporated in this Eighth Commandment.

Property

God speaks about the right of people to own and to hold property. In the ultimate sense of the matter, we recognize that the Bible teaches ownership is a divine prerogative. In Haggai 2:8 God says, "The silver is mine, and the gold is mine, saith the Lord of hosts." Psalm 24:1: "The earth is the Lord's and the fulness thereof; the world, and they that dwell therein." What those and other verses in the Bible teach is that God is the owner of everything, from beginning to end. He owns "the cattle on a thousand hills." God has this whole world in His hands. All you and I have really have has been lent to us as a gift of God. In 1 Timothy 6:7 the Bible says, "For we brought nothing into this world, and it is certain that we can carry nothing out." So, we must establish, first of all, that in the matter of property, in the matter of ownership, God is the initial and final Divine Owner.

Not only is there the principle of *ownership*, we must also establish the principle of *trusteeship*. The Bible teaches that God does place property in trust—material things—to individuals. We are merely the tenants on the farm. Perhaps some of you have had an experience similar to mine. My grandfather was a tenant farmer. Without owning it, he just tilled the land for someone else, and he shared in the profits and benefits of that land. The Bible establishes that you and I are to be tenants for God. God has ownership; we have trusteeship. We are responsible to Him to be faithful to administer the possessions God has placed in our hands. With that broad understanding—that ultimately everything belongs to God, and that you and I are merely trustees of what God has let us have for a short time—the Bible also sets forth the right of individuals to own property.

The Bible does not teach communism. Some use the example in the Book of Acts—of the early believers as they shared things and "had all things common"—as proof of communism. Yet, you will discover that it was never repeated again in the New Testament. That people still have the right to possess property is not contrary to the teachings of Scripture. For instance, when Ananias and Sapphira began to admire what Barnabas had done, as he took all he had, sold it, and brought the proceeds to the church, they decided to emulate him. Yet, because of their selfishness and desire to hold back, they kept back part of it. Simon Peter said to them, "While it [was in your possession], was it not [yours]?" (Acts 5:4). He was establishing the right of individuals to possess property, to have things which belong to them.

In Deuteronomy 27:17 I want to show you a statement and point out a word in that verse. "Cursed be he that removeth his neighbor's landmark." Circle that word *landmark*. What is the meaning of the word, *landmark*? In the Old Testament, when the children of Israel entered the land God had promised them, He measured out and distributed among them certain property. For instance, the last half of the Book of Joshua is a geographical manual for the distribution of the land of Israel—God giving the land to the people. So, they established landmarks. One's landmark established the property which was his. It was his by right. God had given it to him. God has established certain landmarks in our lives as well. Every individual is entitled to certain domestic joys. A landmark. God has established the right to the ownership of property. That is why God says, "Thou shalt not steal." It is a matter of the ownership of property.

Dishonesty

Stealing is embedded in the heart of every person. All of us are born with that innate tendency to want something which doesn't belong to us. It affects all ages, the young as well as the old. It isn't long until that little baby wants to reach over to the neighbor's baby, pull that pacifier out of its mouth, and stick it in its own. The little thief has already started stealing something that belongs to someone else. Old folks still have the temptation to reach over and grab something that doesn't belong to them. All classes are afflicted with the sin of dishonesty. All races are afflicted—red and yellow, black and white, all are thieves within His sight! It also affects all classes. Not only do the poor steal, but the rich also steal. God says, "Thou shalt not steal." He is dealing with the matter of dishonesty. For purposes of this message I have laid out a threefold category of stealing for the purposes of classification. I want to talk about *simple stealing, sophisticated stealing,* and *spiritual stealing.*

Simple Stealing

Simple stealing is easy. All of us understand it. In the newspaper yesterday I picked up five articles: "Boys charged with stealing auto." Two boys, ages fifteen and seventeen, were charged with grand theft of an auto. "Salesman accused of stealing items." A salesman has been charged with stealing $2,000 in electronics from the store where he worked—four videocassette recorders, camcorders, two compact disc players, and a phone-answering machine. "Cash stolen from a home." A burglar stole $165 in cash from a wallet while the home's occupant was asleep. Simple stealing—"Motel guest's suitcase robbed." A burglar broke into a hotel room, stole a guest's suitcase containing a thousand dollars. That's simple stealing. "Satellite receiver reported stolen." A $20,000 satellite receiver was stolen from a wooded area in Palm Valley. Everybody knows that's stealing and a violation of the Commandment that says, "Thou shalt not steal." In other words, the man who puts a mask on his face, puts a gun in his pocket, walks into a bank with a sack in his hand, and steals money from that bank is a robber. He is a burglar; he has stolen.

I heard about a policeman interviewing a bank teller who had been robbed three times by the same person. The policeman asked, "Did you notice anything special about the robber?" "Oh, yes, he seemed to be better dressed each time!"

Once a guy walked into a bank, wrote out a note, and passed it to the teller. The note said, "This is a holdup, give me all your cash." The teller hardly looked up and said, "Straighten your tie, stupid, they're taking your picture." God's candid camera in heaven is taking the pictures, and when God says "Thou shalt not steal," He is keeping a record of those who do.

Then we move to another area of simple stealing—shoplifting. A person goes into a store, picks up an item, and takes it out of the store without paying. The U.S. Department of Commerce has estimated that about 35 million people actually do that undetected while there are 5 million who are caught shoplifting. That is why businesses have had to take all kinds of precautions to stop shoplifting. There are cameras, security systems, store detectives, electronic devices even on pieces of clothing. That is why when you walk by the fur department in a store, you will notice they have been chained and locked so nobody can walk out with one. They estimate that at least one in every fifty-two customers in the average American business attempts or succeeds in shoplifting, stealing something out of that store without paying.

A member of my congregation in Mobile, Alabama, a top executive of one of the leading department stores in America, said that the chain routinely, right on the top of what you and I pay for our merchandise, must assess a certain percentage increase to cover the amount of goods that would be stolen from their company every year. Shoplifting is a clear-cut example of why "Thou shalt not steal."

Let's look at sophisticated stealing. Stealing can become far more sophisticated than that. A guy who walks into a bank with a mask on his face and a gun in his hand is called a simple burglar, but the bank employee who steals from his bank is an embezzler. A person who goes to a government facility and steals is called a thief. When a congressman or senator misuses the money of the nation—that's called "misappropriation of funds." We have different words for sophisticated stealing. We talk about "white-collar crime," "fraud," "insider trading." In the world of business all kinds of sophisticated stealing are perpetrated. "False advertising." Consider all the outfits which advertise products incorrectly for a wrong impression. False advertising is a sophisticated form of stealing. Or think about the employer who works people and does not pay them a fair wage. God inveighs against crooks like that. God says in James 5:4: "Behold, the hire of the laborers who have reaped down your fields, which is of you kept back by fraud, crieth: and the cries of them which have reaped are entered into the ears of the Lord of sabaoth." God is vitally concerned whether or not you are honest in your dealings with those you employ or those for whom you work.

There was a dentist in one of my churches that committed his life anew and afresh to the Lord. One of his first actions was on Monday morning when he gathered all his employees together— nurses and receptionists—and he said, "We're going to start a Bible study. We'll have a time of Bible reading and prayer to begin our day, and I'm going to give every one of you a raise." That is an indication a man has had a real revival when he begins to pay the kind of wages he ought to pay them. It is stealing for a person to work people and not recompense them fairly for the work they render. On the other side there is a practical balance in the Bible, teaching that in business not only is an employer to pay a fair wage for labor rendered, but also for an employee to return a fair amount of work for salary received. It works both ways. It is stealing from your employer not to give him eight hours of work for an eight-hour salary. People who come in late, leave early, and take excessive breaks and lunches seem to be saying, "How little can I do, and how much can I get paid, and how many benefits are in it for me?" are basically stealing from their employer. They are stealing time.

Stealing of goods. I heard about a CEO with an airplane firm who decided he was going to have a group photograph made of all who worked for him. When they heard that they were all to gather in a certain place, they panicked. They thought it was an inspection. The picture could not be taken until all of the stolen goods the people had dropped on the parking lot were removed. Have you been taking something that doesn't belong to you on the job? That's stealing.

The matter of paying income tax. Jesus taught that we are to pay our income tax. Jesus said in Luke 20:25: "Render therefore unto Caesar the things [that belong unto] Caesar." In Romans 13:7 the Bible says we are to give to "all their dues: tribute to whom tribute is due, custom to whom custom" We are to pay our income tax. It's a form of stealing when we do not pay our income taxes.

Another sophisticated means of stealing is cheating in school, stealing answers from another student, copying answers you do not know and claiming those answers as yours, purloining someone else's ideas and claiming them for yourself. This is also done in other ways besides cheating in school. The Christian needs to be sensitive to copyright laws concerning cassettes and tapes, sheet music, books, and other published and printed material. We must not violate the Commandment which says "Thou shalt not steal." It is plagiarism when you steal somebody else's idea. If a person writes a book or term paper and they lift someone else's ideas in part or full, that's plagiarism. That is stealing.

I heard about a football player who was cheating in school. Of course, not all football players cheat. I'm not picking on football players. This one was unusually dumb. Not all football players are dumb, of course. Some are very bright. He was sitting next to the number-one student in the school, a Phi Beta Kappa. The teacher became a little suspicious because their answers were very similar. The teacher knew that the football player wasn't that smart. Then the teacher knew plenty was wrong when both test papers came in, and the Phi Beta Kappa on question ten wrote, "I don't know the answer." And the football player on that same question put, "Me neither."

When you cheat, what you really do is cheat yourself. You are given credit for a level of attainment which you have not really achieved, and you are going to pay for it in life when you are totally unprepared for what you are trying to do.

Simple Stealing. Sophisticated stealing. Now, there is a third category. Think about *spiritual stealing*. "Thou shalt not steal." In that category I put gossip and slander. When you steal a person's good name, you have stolen just as surely as if you had stolen their automobile—to snatch away a person's good name by an innuendo or statement. I feel for the celebrities of this country. Some of them *are* scoundrels. Others are not. These scandal sheets and all of these sleazy books try to steal the good name of individuals and rob them of their good character, planting the seeds of doubt in the minds of people. That is stealing.

I think about Absalom and what he did. Absalom stole the hearts of the people his own father was supposed to lead. That is a form of stealing. There is another form of stealing—spiritual stealing—and that's when an individual steals from God.

Turn to Malachi 3:8–10. "Will a man rob God? Yet ye have robbed me. But yet ye say, Wherein have we robbed thee? In tithes and offerings." God says you can steal by stealing tithes from Him. That's 10 percent of your income. I knew an oral surgeon who became turned on for the Lord when we were in our stewardship emphasis. He came to me and inquired, "Preacher, should you tithe before or after taxes?" I answered, "Tithe before taxes; God gets more that way." The question is not how little can you give God, but, how much can you give God? To some Christians it's an absolute disgrace if all they ever give to God is the tithe. It's not the amount you write on the check; it's how much that's left in the bank account. That's what really matters. Yet, there are Christians who have stolen from God; they haven't returned at least the tithe to God.

One time when I was pastor in a country church I was really preaching. I said, "Some of you are not giving God His tithe. God's going to get His tithe. He may take it out in flat tires, but he's going to get it." Would you believe I walked out of church that night and my car had a flat tire? I've never said that again!

The point is: when you don't give God 10 percent of your income the Bible says you are stealing from God. You are stealing from the very One in whose hand is your breath. You are so totally dependent on God that you must depend on Him to draw the next breath. Just breathe out for a moment and hold it. Sooner or later you have to take another breath. That next breath is from God. Are you going to rob from the One who holds your very breath in His hand?

Then He says "tithes and offerings." That means giving above the 10 percent, moving into the area of having an offering to give the Lord. We give God the tithe. That's what He expects, but we give to God the offering as an expression of our gratitude. How can we who know the cross life, who have the wonderful Lamb of God, do less than give God a tithe and then an offering on top of that?

We have talked about the right to own property and to have

possessions. We have also dealt with dishonesty, the root of the Commandment, "Thou shalt not steal."

Integrity

All of these negative Commandments have a positive expression. When the Bible says, "Thou shalt not steal," the positive of that is the statement of our Lord when He said, "Do to others as you would have them do to you" (Luke 6:31, NIV). The positive of that is in Romans 13:8 where it says "Owe no man anything, but to love one another." The negative "Thou shalt not steal"; the positive: "Thou shalt love one another."

Turn to Ephesians 4. There are three ways you can get things. You can get things by stealing, by working for them, or by some one giving them to you. In verse 28 I want to show you that those three ways are dealt with in that verse of Scripture. Here he is setting forth for us basic integrity, basic honesty: "Let him that stole, steal no more." Quit your stealing; be honest! It is not nearly so important how much money you make as it is how you make it.

Someone asked the reclusive billionaire, Howard Hughes, "How much money does it take to make a man happy?" His answer was a classic: "Just a little bit more." God counsels us to be honest. Be honest in how you gain what you do. Don't steal. Stay on a budget. A budget is not intended to tell you where your money is; it's to tell you where your money is to go.

Our young couples had a retreat recently. Judge A. C. Soud shared with the men about how expensive it is to obtain a divorce. I think he may have saved a lot of marriages because a bunch of them decided they cannot afford a divorce. One of the problems young couples have is the matter of finances. Learn to operate on a budget. Write it down. Then, learn to make wise investments. There is no such thing as a get-rich scheme. The Bible says "Let him that stole, steal no more."

Industry—"let him labor, working with his hands the thing which is good." There is nothing dishonorable in hard work. Work itself is not a result of the curse of sin. Before sin entered into the Garden of Eden, God directed the man to tend and dress the garden. Jesus was a carpenter. He was not a little namby-pamby, soft-handed kind of a person. He was a carpenter who could pick up those beams of wood and could drive the nails with the hammer. Jesus Christ knew what it was to work.

Learn to work. Work for what you get. Don't expect a hand-out in life. Don't expect people to put it on a platter for you. Work hard. Employers all over this country are wanting to hire people who are willing to work. If you are willing to work, you can normally find a place of employment. You may not start off as the president of the company, but if you will hang in there and work, who knows?

Honesty—"Let him that stole, steal no more." Industry—"rather let him labor, working with his hands the thing which is good." Generosity—"that he may have to give to him that needeth." In other words, you should work hard and provide for your own needs and have a little left over to help somebody else who is less fortunate than you. Learn to be generous. If you will learn to be generous, if you will learn to give to others, and do it "as unto the Lord," you will never be able to outgive God. I don't care what size shovel you have, as you begin to shovel out and give to others as unto the Lord, God has a bigger shovel, and He will pour back into your life and meet the needs of your life.

Zacchaeus climbed up that tree. The Lord asked him to come down. He came down, and that's why the sycamore tree has been slick ever since. He came scooting down that sycamore tree, and Jesus invited himself, "Zacchaeus, I want to eat dinner with you today." Wouldn't you like to have been a fly on the wall and listened to Jesus' words to Zacchaeus that day. We don't know everything that was said but, when it was all over, Zacchaeus said before everybody, "Lord, if I have taken anything wrongfully from anybody [and he had—he was a crooked tax collector] I'll restore it fourfold." Then, Jesus said, "Today is salvation come to this house" (See Luke 19: 1–10). Repentance makes you right with God. Restitution makes you right with your fellowman. "Thou shalt not steal."

Perhaps some of you have committed the greatest theft of all time. The robbery you have committed is more far-reaching than the Brink's robbery. The Bible says, "ye are not your own; ye are bought with a price." For you to keep your life away from the

Savior, who loved you enough to shed His blood on Calvary to purchase you unto Himself, is to commit the greatest robbery that could ever be committed.

Wouldn't you like to give your life to Christ?

9

Some Liars I Have Known

(v. 16)

As I first preached this message, the book by Kitty Kelly entitled *Nancy Reagan, The Unauthorized Biography* hit the bookstores and skyrocketed to number one on the best-seller list. It created quite a sensation because it was a frontal attack on the wife of a past President, Ronald Reagan.

Those who reviewed the book had varying viewpoints. Some claimed that the documentation was rather inadequate and that the sources of the book were questionable, to say the least. Many in the field of writing and journalism questioned the very methodology of Kelly's book. It seemed to be another in the genre of literature known as "trash biography." The question is, "Who was telling the truth?" Was Kelly telling the truth or were the people who were denying her allegations telling the truth? I do not know. You do not know. I have my own opinion.

I also have the opinion that many people today are willing to do, say, or write anything to make a dollar. It is a sad day when people are willing to exploit those who have blessed and helped our country, and try to pull them down by this kind of sleazy journalism. As I was thinking about Kelly's book, a verse of Scripture came to my mind. The last chapter of Revelation, the 15th verse. It talks about those who are going to be outside the city of God. Among those people will be those who love a lie and who make a lie. I had not noticed that combination before, but the verse says those who love a lie and those who make a lie. There seems to be something about us that causes us to either want to tell a lie or to want to hear a lie. In fact, we have a whole new field of journalism and writing and publication today—the scandal sheet. They are absolutely ridiculous—the tabloids you see in the grocery stores and other places. Some of the things you read are absurd. You read headlines like this: Hundred-year-old woman gives birth to two-headed baby. People buy these kinds of things and read them, and they are somehow tantalized at the thought of hearing the latest dirt, the latest garbage, the latest smut on some person.

The ninth commandment is a commandment from God which says, "Thou shalt not bear false witness against thy neighbor." Simply God is saying, "Thou shalt not lie." This commandment safeguards the reputation of the individual. There is a difference between character and reputation. Your character is one thing; your reputation is another. Character is what you really are. Reputation is what people say you are. Of course, you and I would agree that character is more important than reputation. It is far more important what God knows to be true about you than what people think they know to be true about you. Character is what the angels say before the throne of God. Reputation is what they chisel on your tombstone. Character is more important, but reputation is also important. The Bible says in the Book of Proverbs, "A good name is to be chosen rather than great riches" (Prov. 22:1). It is a terrible sin for a person to tell a lie about another individual—either to say or write something that does damage to the reputation of another person.

In preparing this message, as I began to dig into the Word on the subject of lying, I became overwhelmed at all the Bible really has to say about it, so much so that I cannot possibly put it all together. So I merely put down a number of verses of Scripture. The Bible informs us that God hates lying. Proverbs 6:16 says there are six things that God hates, and that seven are an abomination. Among those seven are "a lying tongue" and "a false witness that speaketh lies" (vv. 17,19). In Proverbs 12:22 the Scriptures say, "Lying lips are abomination to the Lord." In Proverbs 18:21: "Death and life are in the power of the tongue."

That is certainly true. By means of the tongue, by means of the gift of language which God has given us, we are able to speak words that will build, bless, and encourage. We are also able to tear down, do damage, and harm greatly. God hates lying. In spite of that fact, it seems to be the modus operandi of our society. It seems that in every imaginable area lying has become a commonly accepted method of operation. Some advertisers lie in order to sell their products. Some politicians lie in order to garner votes. Some newspapers lie in order to sell papers. It is a common form of activity and communication, and many people accept it as the norm. Yet, when you study what God reveals in the Word you will discover that God severely condemns lying. The Ninth Commandment is, "Thou shalt not bear false witness against thy neighbor"— you must not lie.

Having considered that as an introduction I also want to point out that all of us are liars. Our very natures are prone to telling lies. Psalm 58:3 says, "The wicked are estranged from the womb; they go astray as soon as they be born, speaking lies." Do you remember the first lie you ever told? I daresay you do not. All of us start lying at an early age. We become accomplished liars soon in our careers. Do you remember the last lie you told? Was it today? Was it yesterday? Sometime last week? All of us are liars.

One fascinating reality about the war in the Persian Gulf was the "smart bombs." I never realized that we had that kind of technology until now. Smart bombs—bombs that were computer-directed so they could pick out military installations and hit places on a pinpoint. What if God had some smart bombs, and He had directed them toward us? Suppose God's smart bombs were keyed in so they would drop red paint over every person that had ever told a lie? I wonder when the smart bombs fell how many of us would be unstained. We can all identify with this. It is our nature to tell things that are not true. A lie is not difficult to define. A lie is a statement of untruth with the intention to deceive—a statement which is contrary to fact and told intentionally to deceive.

My subject is "Some Liars I Have Known." I'm going to share some of the liars I've known along the way. First of all I want to define lying.

Let's *Define* Lying

What is the origin of lying? In John 8:44 the Lord Jesus Christ tells us the origin of lying. "Ye are of your father the devil." That blows to smithereens the doctrine of the universal Fatherhood of

God and the brotherhood of man. There are two families in this world. There is the family of God, and there is the family of the devil. "And the lusts of your father ye will do. He was a murderer from the beginning, and abode not in the truth, because there is no truth in him. When he speaketh a lie, he speaketh of his own: for he is a liar and the father of it." Lies originate from the devil because he is a liar, and he is the originator of lies. You may recall that in the Garden of Eden the devil lied about God to man. He said to man, "Ye shall not surely die: For God doth know that in the day thereof, . . . and ye shall be as gods" (Gen. 3:4–5). The devil lied to man about God.

In the Book of Job, God inquired of the devil, "Hast thou considered my servant Job? that there is none like him on the earth?" The devil said, "Skin for skin. . . . touch his [body] and he will curse thee to thy face" (2:3–5). The devil was lying to man about God. Then in the New Testament there were those false witnesses who came forth with slanderous lies about the Lord Jesus Christ and were responsible for His crucifixion. All truth comes from God. All lies come from the devil. So the devil puts these lies in our hearts. The devil causes us to lie. In Acts 5 we are given the account of Ananias and Sapphira in the early church. They lied about what they had sold their property for and lied about the amount of money they laid before the apostles. Simon Peter lowered the boom on them, "Why hath Satan filled thine heart to lie to the Holy Ghost?" It is the role of the devil to fill our hearts with lies. So, when you and I lie we are more like the devil than we are like the Lord Jesus Christ. Jesus is "the true and faithful witness." The devil is the untrue and unfaithful witness. So when we lie we put ourselves in bad company. We align ourselves with the devil. We align ourselves with his angels. We align ourselves with those who were responsible for crucifying Jesus Christ on the cross of Calvary.

The Bible also tells us how lies *operate*.

First John 1:6 shows us how lies operate in the human personality. "If we say that we have fellowship with him, and walk in darkness, we lie, and do not the truth." There John declares we tell lies to others. We twist the truth. We lie. We tell untruths. Lies operate by our lying to other people. Verse 8: "If we say that we have no sin [if we say we have no sin nature], we deceive ourselves, and the truth is not in us." We lie to other people, and then we begin to lie to ourselves. We become walking, living lies. Psychologists use a term to explain what they mean when people try to excuse and rationalize themselves. They use the terminology "defense mechanism." Defense mechanisms are devices by which we try to avoid reality—those ways we try to delude and deceive ourselves. How many people lie to themselves? How many people are a walking lie?

Verse 10 says, "If we say we have not sinned we make him a liar, and his word is not in us." We lie to God. The greatest lie any person can ever tell is that they do not need Jesus Christ as their personal Savior. If you have never been saved, and you have the idea you do not need Christ, that you do not need the application of His precious shed blood at Calvary for your sin atonement, you are living in the worst deception and delusion of any person on the earth. But we begin to lie to God and tell Him, "I don't need You."

Then we define lying as to its *outcome*. The Bible shows us the outcome of lying. Oh, the damage lying does! Psalm 52:2—"[Lies are] like a sharp razor [they cut]." Psalm 55:21—"[Lies are like] drawn swords [they pierce]." Psalm 120:4—"[Lies are] sharp arrows of the mighty [they penetrate]." James 3:8—"The tongue . . . is an unruly evil, full of deadly poison." It's like a poisonous snake that slips through the grass unnoticed, strikes suddenly, deposits its deadly poison, and moves away.

It's an old, familiar story. A man had been lied about by another man and had been severely harmed and damaged. As the man was dying the man who had lied about him was called to his bedside. At the bedside the liar said, "I realize I did damage to you, and I'm so sorry I have lied to you. I want you to forgive me."

The dying man replied, "Yes, I'll forgive you for lying on me, but I want you to take my pillow and rip it open, go to the window, and empty the pillow of all of the feathers."

So the man who had lied, somewhat quizzically, did as he was asked. He ripped open the pillow and let all of the feathers out the window. He came back to the dying man and reported, "I have done what you asked me to do."

Then the dying man said, "Sir, go now and recover all of the feathers that you have thrown out the window."

The other man protested, "That would be impossible. There's no way I can recover all of those feathers."

The dying man said, "Likewise, though I forgive you, there is no way you can recover all of the damage that your lying words have done."

Oh, the hearts that have been damaged. Oh, the lives that have been hurt. Oh, the reputations that have been marred by untruthful, slanderous, unkind words. That's the outcome of lying.

There's another outcome of lying—the judgment it ushers in. Matthew 12:37 says, "By thy words thou shalt be justified, and by thy words thou shalt be condemned." In judgment we are going to give an account of our words. About every lie we have spoken, we must give an account to God. Your lying is going to catch up with you sooner or later.

Revelation 21:8 says: "All liars, shall have their part in the lake which burneth with fire and brimstone: which is the second death." That's the ultimate destiny of all unrepentant liars.

Let's *Describe* Lying

Lying has many faces. Lying has many children in its family. Sad to say, some of the offspring are in churches. I want to share with you some liars I have known.

There are those who lie by slandering—slandering is malicious untruth with the intention of doing harm. Psalm 101:5 says: "Whoso privily slandereth his neighbor, him will I cut off." Jesus Christ endured slander when He walked on this earth. They spread slanderous garbage about our Savior, even about His very birth. Jesus Christ lived all of His ministry under the shadow of slander that He had been born illegitimately.

They broadcast a slander on Jesus that ultimately became the testimony which condemned Him to die. Jesus said at one time, "Destroy this temple [talking about His body], and in three days [I'll bring it back from the dead]" (John 2:19). But they slandered Jesus. A malicious untruth about the words of Jesus was batted around. They slandered Him to say that He had claimed He would destroy the Jerusalem temple, the most sacred spot among the

Jewish people. On the basis of that slander our Savior was nailed to a cross. So Jesus knew what it was to be despised and rejected of men. The Bible records that Jesus said, "Blessed are ye, when men shall . . . say all manner of evil against you falsely, for my sake" (Matt. 5:11). Oh, that old slanderer in the family of lies; that person who intentionally tells a lie to do harm and damage to an individual.

There are some other liars I have known. I have known those who lie by talebearing. The talebearer tells something, not knowing whether or not their facts are correct. They tell something, but they don't check the facts to find out if this is true.

Listen to the Word of God. Leviticus 19:16—"Thou shalt not go up and down as a talebearer among thy people." First Timothy 5:13—"And withal they learn to be idle, wandering about from house to house, and not only idle but tattlers also and busy bodies, speaking things which they ought not." Sometimes the talebearer takes the form of a rumormonger. He's the one who spreads an innuendo. Some people seem to have a keen sense of rumor. Somehow they seem to enjoy spreading things. Ever heard this: "They say"? The things "they say." I have followed this policy pretty much through my ministry. When somebody says something I say, "Give me their name. I want to check this out to be sure it is true."

What about gossips? Gossips are the verbal pests of society: buzzing, swarming, striking, kicking, stinging, and hurting. What is it about us that enjoys hearing gossip? By the way, what you enjoy hearing will inevitably come to you. It does not compliment you that people feel free to share their gossip with you. Let me remind you that those who gossip to you will gossip about you. Yet, people talk about hearing juicy gossip. The worst form of gossip I know is this "spiritual gossip." "I don't want to say anything that will hurt, but I want to give you something to pray about." We attach spiritual terminology to it. People like to get hold of that juicy gossip and like an orange squeeze out all the juice out of the tale. Talebearers carrying stories from other people.

Proverbs 18:8—"The words of a talebearer are as wounds, and they go down into the innermost parts of the belly." Proverbs

26:20—"Where no wood is, there the fire goeth out: so where there is no talebearer, the strife ceases." That is exactly right. Why don't you make up your mind tonight that you will never be a part of any gossip in the fellowship of First Baptist Church. Make up your mind you will never be a part of the rumormongers who spread their tales and tattle from place to place and person to person. I don't think we have a whole lot of that in our church, but I'm sure we have some with 22,000 members.

One ancient writer said that the tattler and those who listen to gossip both ought to be hanged: the tattler by his tongue; those who listen by their ears.

Then there are those who lie by whispering. Romans 1:29–30 talks about the whisperers and the backbiters. Second Corinthians 12:20 says, "For I fear, lest, when I come, I shall not find you such as I would, and that I should be found unto you such as you would not: lest there be . . . backbitings, whispering." Whisperers are those who get behind the backs of people, those who silently, secretly whisper their little stories. Backbiters are those who don't have the courage to say something face to face with an individual. They are all smiles to their face and then they get behind their back and they stab them in the back. God have mercy on the whisperers. God have mercy on the backbiters and the backstabbers.

There are some other liars I have known—those who lie by insinuating. You can lie by saying very little. You can lie with just a word. "Isn't she a sweet Christian person?" "Well." "She's such a wonderful Christian." "Oh?" "What do you think about this brother who has just joined our church?" "Well, I just don't want to say anything." You can lie by asking a question. "Who does she think she is?" Proverbs 6:12–13—"A naughty person, a wicked man, walketh with a froward mouth. He winketh with his eyes, he speaketh with his feet, he teacheth with his fingers." Sometimes you don't even have to say a word—just a knowing nod. Just a silent shrug. Just the arching of the eyebrows. Just the tone of voice. Do you remember what the enemies of Jesus said in John 8:41? When they said about Jesus and themselves; "We be not born of fornication," it was the same old lie. They were saying we weren't born of fornication, but He certainly was. I've known some who lie by their insinuations, by the inflection of their voices, by the appearance of their faces. God have mercy on liars.

Then there are some other liars I have known. I have known those who lie by flattering. Proverbs 26:28 says: "A flattering mouth worketh ruin." Flattering is the giving of insincere praise. There is certainly an appropriate time for legitimate praise. It is certainly correct and right for us to show genuine appreciation. We probably do not praise people enough. We probably do not show as much appreciation for people as we ought to show. Flattery is something altogether different. Flattery is insincere praise. Flattery is saying something to someone's face that you wouldn't think of saying behind their back. Think about that. "That's the prettiest dress you have on, Darling. You are lovely." Then you walk away saying, "That fat pig. She looks like a mess." "God bless you, Brother, that's a wonderful Sunday School lesson you taught." You walk away saying, "That's the dullest thing I ever listened to." That's flattery. You had better watch the flatterer.

Listen to Psalm 55:21—"The words of his mouth were smoother than butter, but war was in his heart. His words were softer than oil, yet they were drawn swords." Flattery is like perfume. It's all right to smell it, but don't swallow it. Man is the only animal I know that when you pat him on the back, his head swells. We all love flattery. I've been in the ministry a long time, and I've had flattery and I've had praise, and I've been thankful for the praise when it comes. I've had criticism. But I have learned to pass the flattery and the praise and the criticism on to Jesus. If there is any praise, I just pass it on to Jesus. If there is any criticism, I just pass it on to Jesus. If the criticism is true, then Jesus can help me learn from it. If the criticism is unjust and untrue, then I just pass it on to Jesus. You are probably as bad as some people think you are and not nearly as good as you think you are. If everybody knew everything about me that God knows about me they would criticize me far more than they do anyhow. I'd probably get what I deserved. Some liars I have known.

There are some who tell lies by condoning. Not that you tell a lie, but you allow people in your presence to say things that are unkind, untrue, and malicious about another individual. By your silence you give consent to what they have to say. You'd better be very careful that you don't just stand by and let someone damage the reputation of another and do verbal harm to an individual and never stand up for the person who is being maliciously mistreated. Some liars I have known.

Let's *Defeat* Lying

Every one of these Commandments that are cast in the negative mode can be placed in a positive. When God says, "Thou shalt not commit adultery," you could make this positive by saying, "Thou shalt be sexually pure." When God says, "Thou shalt not steal," you can put it positively by saying, "Thou shalt be honest, thou shalt work, thou shalt be generous." When the Bible says, "Thou shalt not bear false witness against they neighbor," the positive of that is, "Thou shalt bear true witness for your neighbor." When it says you must not lie, the positive of that is you must tell the truth. This Commandment is founded on the very nature of God. God, the Father, is true. Jesus Christ said, "I am the way, the truth, and the life" (John 14:6). The Holy Spirit is called the Spirit of Truth. This Commandment to be truthful is based on the character of God.

Here are three ways to defeat lying.

We Must Love the Truth

When David was confessing his sin before God—David had admitted lying on top of his murdering and adultery and all of the other things—he said to God, "Thou desireth truth in the inward parts" (Ps. 51:6). It's a problem down inside. The heart of the problem is the problem of the heart. Jesus said out of the abundance of the heart, the mouth speaketh. Jeremiah 17:9 says, "The heart is deceitful above all things, and desperately wicked." It is our nature to tell that which is not true. We need a change of nature. When people, by nature, lie they become so accustomed to lying they don't even realize they are lying. It becomes habit-forming. It's just a part of them to tell that which is not true. You need a change in your heart.

I was reading in 2 Thessalonians 2:10 where it says concerning the time of the Antichrist—"They received not the love of the truth, that they might be saved." If you turn that around it means that when you are saved you love the truth. If you will love the truth, if you will receive the love of the truth—the truth that you are a sinner and in need of a Savior, the truth that Jesus Christ died on the cross to save you from your sins, the truth that you can be saved from your sins if you will receive the love of the truth— then you will have truth in the inward parts. You will learn to love the truth.

Learn the Truth

As we study God's word we acquaint ourselves with truth. Ephesians 4:21—"If so be that you have heard him, and have been taught by him, as the truth is in Jesus." Philippians 4:8—"Whatsoever things are true, . . . think on these things." After you come to Christ as your Savior you are to fill your mind and your heart with God's truth. You are to learn truth and to learn that which is true from God's Holy Word and stand in the truth and be committed to the truth.

Live the Truth

Ephesians 4:25—"Wherefore putting away lying, speak every man truth with his neighbor; for we are members one of another." Ephesians 4:15—"Speaking the truth in love." Commit yourself to be a truthful person. Love the truth, learn the truth, and then just live the truth. As you grow in your Christian life, every time you tell something that is not the truth the Holy Spirit will convict you and you immediately confess it before the Lord. That's why you desperately need the Lord Jesus. Revelation 21:27 says, "There shall no wise enter into it any thing that . . . maketh a lie." There will be no liars in heaven.

I've just said that we are all liars. Is there any hope? The good news is that Christ can forgive us of our sins. He can change our nature, which tends toward lying, and give us a nature that tends toward telling the truth.

I used to have a radio program in the early years of my ministry. The radio station had a piece of equipment that would erase everything on both sides of a tape if you rubbed it on both sides. What a beautiful illustration of the blood of Jesus

Christ! We bring these lying tongues of ours to the Lord Jesus. We bring these hearts of ours that love and make a lie, and the blood of Jesus Christ cleanses us from all sin.

Wouldn't you like a Savior like that?

10
Don't Want What
Belongs to Somebody Else

(v. 17)

In the Persian Gulf War, shortly before the launching of the ground attack, Saddam Hussein, the butcher of Baghdad, said that it was going to be the mother of all battles. It was not, but that's what he called it. Sometime after that President Bush introduced his wife as the mother of all Bushes. That was certainly more true than what Saddam said about the mother of all battles.

This Commandment can appropriately be titled "the mother of all sins." As we study this Tenth Commandment, "Thou shalt not covet," you will discover that indeed this is the sin that produces all of the other sins. You will immediately notice that there is a difference between the tenth and the previous nine. The previous nine are primarily outward. The tenth is inward. The first nine have to do with sins of the actions. This one has to do with the sin of the attitude. The first nine are primarily about deeds. This one is a matter of desire. The first nine are, for the most part, visible. This last of the Ten Commandments is invisible. It is an inward sin that is manifested in all the other nine. In the New Testament the word, *covet*, has as its root meaning to have more. It is really a combination of two words: *have* and *more*. So the word *covet* means to desire to have more. When we think in terms of covetousness we think primarily about money. Of course, people do desire to have more money. In 1 Timothy 6:10 the Bible says "the love of money is the root of all evil which while some have coveted after, they have erred from the faith and have pierced themselves through with many sorrows." So, there are many people who covet material things.

So, the word *covet* means to have more. At the root is the word *desire*. It really is a two-pronged definition, actually. First of all, it is an excessive desire for something you do not have. It is when your desire for something you do not have becomes the ruling passion of your life. Modern words would be *greed* or *materialism*, excessive desire for something you do not have.

There's a second definition. Covetousness is also an envious desire for something which belongs to someone else—a desire to have something that someone else has. The words we would use today would be *jealousy* or *envy*. So, let's talk about the mother of all sins. Excessive desire for what we do not have and envious desire for that which someone else has. It's not primarily money; though money may be a part. In this Commandment the Lord says, "Thou shalt not covet thy neighbor's house, . . . his wife, nor his manservant, nor his maidservant, nor his ox, nor his ass, nor anything that is thy neighbor's." It may be a desire for money, but it may be the desire for many other things as well.

Nor does covetousness merely mean just simple desire. There are some who believe that if you can just eliminate all desire—their goal is the cessation of all desire. For instance, Buddhism teaches a state of mind which a person can reach called Nirvana. They mean that you can get to a certain state of mind where you have no more desire; total cessation of all desire. That's not what God is teaching in this Commandment. God is not saying that there should be no desire. In 1 Corinthians 12:31 the Bible says we are to "covet [spiritual] gifts." In the 14th chapter, the 39th verse, he says we are to "covet to prophesy."

So, there are some things that are perfectly legitimate for us to desire. It is not wrong to desire to have peace of mind; nor is it wrong to want to be happy. It is not wrong to desire those things that you may not have. It is certainly right for a person to desire to obtain an education. It is certainly right for a person to have a desire for a Christian husband or wife. It is right for a person to desire to have personal tranquillity and peace. So, to covet does not mean the cessation of all desire. The mother of all sins is excessive desire for what you do not have or for what someone else has.

I call it the mother of all sins because I think you will find as you go back through the previous nine that all of these sins can be brought to fruition by the sin of covetousness. For instance, the first two tell us we are not to have any other gods before the Lord

God and that we are not to make a graven image. Colossians 3:5 says that covetousness is idolatry. When we put anything before God or when we make a god out of any other thing, then that covetousness causes us to break the first two Commandments. The Third Commandment says we are not to "take the name of the Lord our God in vain." Ananias and Sapphira took the name of the Lord in vain. They lied to the Lord because of the sin of covetousness in their hearts.

The Fourth Commandment says to "Remember the sabbath day, to keep it holy." I wonder how many people in our society violate this Fourth Commandment because of the interior sin of covetousness?

The Fifth Commandment says to "Honor thy father and thy mother." I wonder how many children have neglected the material welfare of their own parents because of the sin of covetousness? "Thou shalt not kill." How many murders have been committed because of covetousness? People kill to take something someone else has. "Thou shalt not steal." Covetousness will cause you to steal what belongs to another person because you have an envious desire to get what that person has. "Thou shalt not bear false witness." Covetousness will cause you to lie about an individual, to steal their reputation, to steal their good name, to take from them something that you wish you had yourself. This is a sin you can commit and your friends will never know you have committed it. Fingerprints won't pick up this sin. Police radar will never catch this sin. This sin cannot be placed on the law books. In order for this sin to be caught you have to take the policeman off the street corner and put him in the heart. This Commandment has to do with the inward condition of the heart.

Let's *Explain* Covetousness

Here are three things about this mother of all sins that help explain its meaning. First of all, covetousness is a heart sin. In Mark 7:21–23 our Lord said: "And [Jesus] said, That which cometh out of the man, that defileth the man. For from within, out of the heart of men, proceed evil thoughts, adulteries, fornications, murders, thefts, covetousness. . . . All these evil things come from within, and defile the man." Covetousness is a matter of the heart.

It is the poisonous plant that is rooted deeply in the heart of every one of us. We are born with a nature that tends to covetousness. Even after you are saved you still have to battle the sin of covetousness. In Ephesians 5:3 it says: "But fornication, and all uncleanness, or covetousness, let it not be once named among you, as becometh saints." It is a problem of the heart that you do not solve even by means of the new birth experience. It is still there. It is a matter of the heart, desiring what you do not have, excessive materialism, envy of what other people have.

Not only is it a heart problem but we learn from the Scriptures that it is a hidden problem. In 1 Thessalonians 2:5 Paul talks about a "cloak of covetousness." That is exactly true. It is one of those sins we tend to cover over. Nobody wants to reveal that they have covetousness in their heart.

The Lord Jesus was teaching on an occasion and the Pharisees were there. In Luke 16:13–14, Jesus taught, "You cannot serve God and mammon. And the Pharisees also, who were covetous, heard all these things and they derided him." Jesus was exposing the covetousness in their hearts. Nobody wants to admit they are covetous. All of us want to hide it.

I have heard some wonderful conversion testimonies. I have heard people give testimony to the fact that they were converted from the sin of alcohol and drunkenness. I have heard people saved from the terrible addictive sins of lust give testimony. I have heard people talk about being saved from bigotry, prejudice, and hatred. But I have never, in all of my ministry, heard anybody stand up and praise God that they were saved from the sin of covetousness. It is a hidden sin, something we tend to nurse and coddle down in our hearts.

According to the Scriptures it is a hideous sin. Think about how hideous it is. In Romans 1:29 Paul painted a full-scale portrait of the human race and the depravity of the human heart: "Being filled with all unrighteousness, fornication, wickedness, covetousness, maliciousness." Did you notice in that list that covetousness is found between maliciousness and wickedness? It is a hideous sin. It is the sin of "idolatry," Colossians 3:5 says. God made the human heart for fellowship with Him. God made the human heart to be occupied by God Himself. When we allow excessive or envious desire to put anything between us and God; to come and occupy the human heart instead of our dear Lord, we have committed the hideous sin of idolatry. It is bowing the knee to anything or anyone rather than bowing the knee to God. Ephesians 5:5 says: "For this ye know, that no whoremonger, nor unclean person, nor covetous man, who is an idolater, hath any inheritance in the kingdom of Christ and of God." He is simply saying that if you are a covetous person you will not enter into the kingdom of God. This sin keeps people from being saved. It really does.

Do you remember the rich young ruler who came to Jesus? What a wonderful young man he was in many respects. The Bible says Jesus looked at him and loved him. He wanted to have eternal life. He said to Jesus, "Master, what good thing shall I do, that I may have eternal life?" Jesus began to list the Commandments. It is interesting to me that Jesus took the second half of the Ten Commandments—those that have to do with our relationships with one another—and He gave all of that second half except the one, "Thou shalt not covet." Do you think Jesus was trying to get his attention? The young man said, "All of these have I kept from my youth up." Then Jesus hit the sore spot in his life. He said, "Sell [everything you have], and give to the poor, . . . and come and follow me." The Bible says that when the young man heard that he was grieved for he had many possessions and he turned and walked away from the Lord Jesus Christ. His covetousness for material things kept him from giving his life to Jesus Christ (see Matt. 19:16–22).

There are people who sit in these services Sunday after Sunday and they know they need Jesus Christ. Yet they hesitate to come forward to receive Christ, follow the Lord in baptism, and become a member of this church fellowship because they are afraid if they do the church is going to want some of their money and they don't want to give up any of their money. This sin of covetousness is a heart sin, a hidden sin, a hideous sin.

Let's *Examine* Covetousness

In Joshua 7 is an Old Testament picture of an experience of covetousness. Let's examine it. Let's see just exactly how covetousness works. Joshua was leading the children of Israel into the land of promise. They had walked around the walls of the city of Jericho and the walls had come tumbling down. Filled with self-confidence they went on up to the city of Ai and were embarrassingly defeated. Joshua got on his knees and said, "Lord, what's wrong?" The Lord said, "Get up off your knees, no time to pray, there's sin in the camp." That sin was the sin of a man named Achan. Here's Achan's confession in verses 20-22. "Indeed I have sinned against the Lord God of Israel and thus and thus have I done: When I saw among the spoils a goodly Babylonish garment, and two-hundred shekels of silver, and a wedge of gold of fifty shekels weight, then I coveted them, and took them; and, behold, they are hid in the earth in the midst of my tent, and the silver under it."

Watch the progression of Achan's sin—the words, "I saw." He saw the silver. He saw the gold. He saw the garments. "Took." He not only had a desire, but he committed a deed. The deception. He hid them in the earth. That is exactly the way the sin of covetousness always works. It starts with a desire. If left untended it will move to a deed and then it will move to deception. In this instance, Achan was trying to deceive other people.

In the New Testament there is picture of covetousness. In Luke 12 a man who had a dispute with a brother came to the Lord Jesus Christ. In verse 13 we are told one of the company said to Jesus: "Master, speak to my brother, that he divide the inheritance with me." They were having a family squabble. Their father had died and they were having a fuss. If you really want to see how covetous people are, let people get in a squabble over an inheritance and you will see human beings become like vicious animals. This covetousness is the mother of all sins. It is a vicious sin indeed. Jesus said in verse 14: "Man, who made me a judge or a divider over you? . . . Take heed, and beware of covetousness: for a man's life consisteth not in the abundance of the things which he possesseth." Then in verses 16–21 He told the parable about the rich fool. The Bible says that the man's land became very prosperous but when the man saw the prosperity of his land, did he see God and was he grateful for God's blessings and God's bounty upon him? Did he see other people that he could help? Did he see an opportunity to take his plenty and share it with those who didn't have very much? No. What did he do? The parable Jesus told that he began to think within himself—that's where it starts—a desire. Then it moves on to a deed. He says: "This will I do: I will pull down my barns and build greater; . . . I will bestow all my fruits and my goods. And I will say to my soul, Soul, thou hast much goods laid up for many years; take thine ease, eat, drink, and be merry." Now he has moved to deception. It started off with a desire. It moved on to a deed. Now, it's moved on to deception. In this instance he is not deceiving others, he is deceiving himself. This man has made some mistakes. This man has mistaken his bank-book for his Bible. This man has the idea that somehow what he has in his checking account is more important than what God has written in the Word about the riches of faith and the riches of spiritual things. He also mistook his body for his soul. He said, "I will say to my soul, . . . eat, drink." You know your soul doesn't eat and drink. It's your body that eats and drinks. There are a lot of people who mistake their body for their soul. They think if they take care of their body, then everything is fine. You can be well cared for physically, but absolutely poverty stricken spiritually. He mistook his body for his soul.

The greatest deception of all is he mistook time for eternity. He said, "I'll say to my soul, soul, . . . eat, take thine ease for many years." Like a clap of thunder the voice of God thundered out of heaven and said to him, "Thou fool, this night thy soul shall be required of thee." He thought he had many years. God said, "Tonight is it. It's all over." A man is a fool who commits the sin of covetousness selling out eternity for a bit of pleasure in time. That's how covetousness always works. A desire, a deed, a deception.

We have explained covetousness. We have examined covetousness.

Let's *Expel* Covetousness

Let's deal with the sin of covetousness. Let's get rid of that mother of all sins. In order to expel covetousness, first of all, there has to be a realization. You have to realize it's there.

Paul was a marvelous example how the law of God worked in his life to show him his desperate need of Jesus Christ. In Romans 7 Paul shares with us how the law of God brought him to the awareness that he needed a Savior. Paul was brought up as an orthodox Jew. At the age of thirteen Paul would have had his bar mitzvah. That means he would become a son of the law, responsible to keep the law of God. Here's his testimony in verses 7–8. "What shall we say then? Is the law sin? God forbid. Nay, I had not known sin but by the law: for I had not known lust, except the law had said, Thou shalt not covet. But sin taking occasion by the commandment, wrought in me all manner of concupiscence. For without the law sin was dead." Paul was saying that he read those nine Commandments and compared his outward life and felt pretty good. Every time Paul would get to that Tenth Commandment—"Thou shalt not covet," he would be troubled in his spirit. He knew down deep in his heart that he had violated the Commandment "Thou shalt not covet." It was the realization that the sin of covetousness was in his heart that showed him that he was lost and he needed a Savior. James 2:10 says if you have not kept all of the Commandments you are guilty of breaking them all. I could probably convince every reasonable person in this building that you have broken all of the Ten Commandments. Let's just suppose I could not convince you that you had broken the first nine. Is there any reasonable, honest person in this building who would say to me that you have never coveted? That you have never had an excessive desire for something you did not have? That you have never had an envious desire for something which someone else had. If you admit that you have broken the Tenth Commandment you are a lost sinner in desperate need of Jesus Christ as your Savior. You must realize that you have broken the Commandment and you need Christ.

We must also resist covetousness. You have received Jesus as your Savior, but you still battle with that sin of covetousness, God says to the believer in Colossians 3:5. The word *mortify* (*mortician* is our word today) means to put to death. A mortician is someone who buries the dead. When he says mortify he is meaning put to death. "Mortify therefore your members which are upon the earth; fornication, uncleanness, inordinate affection, evil concupiscence, and covetousness, which is idolatry." God says to the child of God—"Put the sin of covetousness to death in your heart. When it arises in your heart, put it to death. You just nip it in the bud." How do you put it to death? How do you resist it? All of these Commandments which are placed in a negative mode could also be placed in a positive mode. In Romans 13 we find that clearly laid out for us. "Owe no man anything, but to love one another: for he that loveth another has fulfilled the law. For this, Thou shalt not commit adultery, Thou shall not kill, Thou shalt not steal, Thou shalt not bear false witness, Thou shalt not covet; and if there be any other commandment it is briefly comprehended in this saying, namely, Thou shalt love thy neighbor as thyself" (vv. 8–9). You resist the sin of covetousness by loving your neighbor. You take the positive approach and love your neighbor. If you are loving your neighbor as you ought then you are not coveting that which your neighbor has.

Take parents whose children have now left the home and are married, working, and doing well. Their marriage is faring well. They are working on their jobs and making good incomes. They have bought a house and things are doing fine. Have you ever heard a parent express displeasure in the prosperity of their child? Have you ever heard a parent be upset or alarmed because of the well-being of their child? Absolutely not. They love their children, and they are excited and blessed when they do well. If you and I love people the way we ought to we will not have an excessive, envious desire for that which they do have. We realize it, we resist it, and we replace it.

In Psalm 119:36 the Bible says, "Incline my heart unto thy [commandments], and not to covetousness." We incline our heart to the Word. We incline our heart to God's precepts. We fill our minds and our hearts with God's truth.

Turn to the Book of Hebrews 13:5–6. "Let your conversation [not just your speech—your whole life-style] be without covetousness; and be content with such things as ye have: for he hath said, I will never leave thee nor forsake thee. So that we may boldly say the Lord is my helper, and I will not fear what man shall do unto me." Replace covetousness with contentment in the Lord. We covet because of excessive desire. We want something which we do not have. Discontent is the expression of illegitimate desires. We replace covetousness with contentment in the Lord and learn to look to the Lord to meet the daily needs of our lives. Paul said, "I have learned, in whatsoever state I am, therewith to be content" (Phil. 4:11). Having food and raiment be content. You didn't bring anything into this world, it's certain you are not going to take anything out of it. Learn to get your contentment in Jesus Christ. Epicurus said if you want to make a man happy, add not to his possessions, but take away from his desires. It's great to be content in Jesus. Incline your heart to God's testimonies. You learn to be content in Jesus Christ. "Therefore I thought it necessary to exhort the brethren, that they would go before unto you, and make up beforehand your bounty [gift], whereof ye had noticed before, that the same [gift] might be ready as a matter of bounty, and not as of covetousness" (2 Cor. 9:5). He is saying learn to replace covetousness with generosity. Instead of having your mind always on getting, learn to give. Become a giving person. In learning to give you will learn to expel the mother of all sins from your heart.

It is said that when Alexander the Great had conquered the known world he instructed his officers that when he died his hands were to be left outside the coffin so that all might see that though he had conquered the world he could carry nothing with him into the hereafter. We are born into this world grabbing and grasping, but when we leave this world we die with our hands open and extended. Don't make the mistake of just living your life in constant desire for that which you do not have. Come to Jesus. When you come to Jesus you will find that you have everything that's worth living for. You will have a house eternal in the heavens not made with hands. You will find that you are an heir of God and a joint heir with Jesus Christ. You will find that your name is written in the roll books of glory. You will find that you have an inheritance incorruptible, undefiled, and that fadeth not away.